THE URUGUAY

Sir Richard F. Burton about 1865-1867

JOSÉ BASÍLIO da GAMA

THE URUGUAY
(A Historical Romance of South America)

THE
SIR RICHARD F. BURTON
TRANSLATION

Huntington Library Manuscript HM 27954

Edited, with Introduction,
Notes, and Bibliography, by
Frederick C. H. Garcia
and
Edward F. Stanton

UNIVERSITY OF CALIFORNIA PRESS
Berkeley   Los Angeles   London

The lithograph of Sir Richard F. Burton that appears as
the frontispiece of this volume is reproduced with the per-
mission of the Huntington Library, San Marino, Califor-
nia. Artist and date unknown. The drawing appears at
the beginning of a volume of letters from Sir Richard and
Lady Burton to Leonard Smithers. By comparing this
drawing with other portraits and photographs of Burton,
we can probably date it around 1865-1867, the approxi-
mate time of his translation of *The Uruguay.*

University of California Press
Berkeley and Los Angeles, California

University of California Press, Ltd.
London, England

Copyright © 1982 by The Regents of the University of California

Library of Congress Cataloging in Publication Data

Gama, José Basílio da, 1740-1795.
  The Uruguay (a historical romance of South
America)

    Translation of O Uraguai.
    Bibliography: p. 251
    1. Seven Reductions, War of the, 1754-1756 —
Poetry.   I. Garcia, Frederick C. H.   II. Stanton,
Edward F.   III. Henry E. Huntington Library and Art
Gallery. Manuscript. HM 27954.   IV. Title.
PQ9696.G3U713   1982   869.1   81-15920
ISBN 0-520-04524-6

Printed in the United States of America

1 2 3 4 5 6 7 8 9

CONTENTS

INTRODUCTION

José Basílio da Gama's *O Uraguai* is probably the most nearly
perfect narrative poem of the entire colonial period in Brazil.
Published in 1769, it was also the most important literary work
of its kind in Portuguese after Camoens's *Os Lusíadas,* written
two centuries earlier. *O Uraguai* deals with the War of the
Seven Reductions (1754-1759), called by Gama's translator, Sir
Richard F. Burton, "the Guaranitic or Jesuit war," waged be-
tween the forces of Portugal and Spain on one side, and the
Tupi-Guarani Indians with their Catholic missionaries on the
other. Conceived in the neoclassic spirit, Gama's poem has a
simplicity of design and a clarity of language that have enabled
it to age more gracefully than other works of the same type. But
a degree of emotion, the feeling for the creator's native land,
and the presence of tropical scenery generated a text that goes
well beyond the usual limits of an eighteenth-century poem.
Though the poem is often considered an epic, its values are
essentially lyric: Gama perceived in his American land a rich-
ness of images and forms from which he created an original aes-
thetic vision of the New World and its native inhabitants. In
the pages of the *Uraguai* we see ranks of plumed Guaranis fac-
ing European artillery; overflowing rivers and troops biv-
ouacked in treetops; an Indian warrior crossing the Uruguay
River by night and setting fire to the enemy camp; prophecies
of a native sorceress; the Cleopatra-like suicide of an Indian
maiden; and the hills, valleys, and plains of the South Ameri-
can hinterland covered by pools of blood and bodies of the war
dead, vultures wheeling in the sky.
    Although it contains inevitable echoes of Camoens,

1

Gama's poem managed to sound fresh and unique in its time, as it does two centuries later. The *Uraguai* was as modern as it was possible to be modern in 1769. Its modest dimensions, commensurate with the historical events portrayed, give it a compactness and unity of effect rare in a narrative poem. The number of times it has been printed testifies to the *Uraguai*'s eminence in Brazilian letters; no Luso-Brazilian poem of the time has gone through so many editions.

In the nineteenth century, when Brazil achieved independence from Portugal and its men of letters sought a national symbol, they found such a figure in Gama's Indian warrior. Already recognized for its literary value, the *Uraguai* acquired a new ideological dimension. Brazilian romantics regarded Gama as the creator of a new, autochthonous tradition in the country's growth toward political and artistic freedom. It was at this time that Richard Francis Burton became acquainted with *O Uraguai*.

One of the great men of the nineteenth century and perhaps the most celebrated translator in the history of English literature, Burton served as Her Majesty's consul in Santos between 1865 and 1868. He described the coffee port as a "wretched hole," another one of those "governmental crumbs" that exiled from power a man too independent and outspoken for drawing room diplomacy.[1] An ordinary Foreign Office consul might even have neglected to learn the language of the country, but the translator of the unexpurgated *Arabian Nights* already had a long familiarity with Portuguese when he arrived in Brazil: he had first studied it as a young army officer in Goa some twenty years earlier. He had even tried his hand at translating passages from the *Lusiads*, a poem he would finally publish in 1880, followed by a two-volume study of Camoens

---

[1]Burton to Monckton Milnes (Lord Houghton), 23 October 1865, Lord Houghton Papers, Trinity College Library, Cambridge. See also the letter dated 20 March 1861. (Permission to quote granted by Trinity College Library.)

and a translation of the same poet's *Lyricks*.[2] Burton was one of the great Victorian linguists; he learned some forty languages and dialects (one of them pornography, his detractors said). There can be no doubt that he knew Portuguese extremely well; he translated more works from that tongue than from any other, with the exception of his beloved Arabic. Thus fully conversant with the Portuguese language and its greatest poet, Burton recognized the literary as well as the ideological significance of *O Uraguai*. A desire to translate the poem followed, along with an almost missionary zeal to acquaint the British public with the literature of Brazil.[3]

Like so many of his translations, Burton's rendition of *The Uruguay* is scrupulously honest, yet bold, personal, and vigorous. He was especially practiced at drawing the line between "unendurable inaccuracy and intolerable servility" in rendering a foreign text.[4] His translation of *O Uraguai* represents the sole English version of this poem, but also stands on its own as an original creation. With his pedagogical bent and his compulsion to explain, Sir Richard offered up the poem with preface, biographical and critical appendices, and copious notes. This material, de rigueur in Victorian times, supplies the reader with the facts necessary for understanding the context of *The Uruguay*. Mysteriously, the notes of both Gama and the translator have disappeared from what is apparently the only surviving copy of Burton's manuscript.[5] A consideration of

[2]*Lusiads*, 2 vols. (London: Bernard Quaritch, 1880); *Camoens: His Life and His Lusiads*, 2 vols. (London: Bernard Quaritch, 1881); *Camoens: The Lyricks*, 2 vols. (London: Bernard Quaritch, 1884).

[3]See Burton's Preface to his translation of *The Uruguay*, and his letter "Translations," *The Athenaeum*, no. 2313 (24 February 1872), pp. 241-243.

[4]Quoted in Fawn M. Brodie, *The Devil Drives: A Life of Sir Richard Burton* (New York: W. W. Norton and Co., 1967), p. 279. The authors are indebted to Brodie for her encouragement in preparing this edition of *The Uruguay*.

[5]HM 27954, Huntington Library, San Marino, California. (The library has granted permission to quote from the manuscript and to publish this edition.)

the verse translation, the supplementary prose, and the problem of missing notes will shed light on *The Uruguay* and on the mind of its translator. This in turn will lead to a second, equally fascinating question: Why was Burton's translation not published in his own lifetime? The present edition of his *Uruguay* is the first to appear in print.

THE HISTORICAL SETTING

The subject of José Basílio da Gama's *O Uraguai*, the War of the Seven Reductions, formed part of the centuries-old struggle between the two branches of the Ibero-American family, the Portuguese and the Spanish. The Treaty of Tordesillas (1494) had granted the eastern edge of South America to Portugal, but the southern part of the area, where the modern boundaries of Brazil and Argentina converge around the river Uruguay, remained in dispute for most of three hundred years. Burton refers to these clashes, saying, "Men wish they had a gold ounce for every throat that has been cut in the place."[6] In

---

On 14-15 April 1953, a manuscript entitled "The Uruguay" was advertised as no. 157 in part 3 of the John B. Stetson Collection, to be put on auction at the Parke-Bernet Galleries, New York. It was described as an autograph manuscript, signed by Burton on the first and final pages, a small quarto, bound or laid in a cloth-backed board volume. In spite of the desire by the company (now Sotheby Parke-Bernet) to protect its clients' privacy, the editors have been able to trace the sale of the manuscript to the Fourth Avenue Bookstore, 138 Fourth Ave., New York. The bookstore has informed us that the manuscript was resold almost immediately, but that there is no record of the purchaser. The editors have made a vigorous attempt to locate the manuscript over a period of six months, without success. Burton's scrupulous bibliographer, Norman M. Penzer, did not mention a second version of "The Uruguay" in *An Annotated Bibliography of Sir Richard Francis Burton* (London: A. M. Philpot, 1923). Huntington Library MS 27954 is written in Burton's own hand, and it is unlikely that Sir Richard would have composed two versions of the same work. A second manuscript of "The Uruguay," if one does exist, would certainly clarify the problem of Burton's missing footnotes, discussed below under the heading "The Manuscript and Two Mysteries."

[6]*Letters from the Battle-fields of Paraguay* (London: Tinsley Brothers, 1870), p. 144. Here Burton is referring to Colônia do Sacramento, a fortress related to the events of *O Uraguai.*

the mid-eighteenth century, intermarriage between members of the Portuguese and Spanish royal families favored a truce and a realignment of the South American borders based on realpolitik. The Treaty of Limits (Madrid, 1750) abandoned the Tordesillas line in favor of the principle of *uti possidetis*, giving possession to the occupants of the land. As part of the agreement, Portugal granted to Spain Colônia do Sacramento, which the Spaniards regarded as a menace to their colonies. In compensation, Spain gave Portugal the Sete Povos das Missões, Spanish Jesuit missions, or "reductions," along the left or eastern bank of the Uruguay River, which seemed to threaten Portuguese control of Rio Grande do Sul. The plot of Gama's poem unfolds in this part of the Uruguay basin; thus its title.[7]

The Treaty of Madrid also required the priests and Indians of the missions to move to lands under Spanish rule. The Jesuits and the Tupi-Guaranis bore no great love for the Portuguese, having been exposed to raiding expeditions of *bandeirantes*, or commandos, from São Paulo for decades. Yet the inhabitants of the seven reductions naturally were reluctant to comply with the terms of the new treaty. It would have been quite simple to pack up and leave, but what were they going to do with their tilled soil, their cattle, their churches, and their memories? They had occupied the land for centuries; it mattered little to them whether the king resided in Madrid or Lisbon. The Indians, and apparently their Jesuit leaders as well, were prepared to disobey the European monarchs and fight for the land they considered their own. The action of Gama's work occurs in the region of the missions, at a time when Portuguese and Spanish troops were attempting to enforce the removal of the Jesuits and their indigenous flock.

---

[7]Gama entitled his poem *O Uraguay;* modern Brazilian editions keep the "a" of the second syllable even as they change the "y" to "i" at the end (*Uraguai*). Burton did not use any one form consistently. With so many variants available, each with a shade of time and meaning, the editors have chosen the current Brazilian form when referring to Gama's poem (*O Uraguai*), and the modern English *Uruguay* when referring to Burton's translation, the river, or the region.

The War of the Seven Reductions dragged on for five years, resulting, of course, in the victory of the Portuguese and Spanish over the underarmed Tupi-Guaranis. José Basílio da Gama's *O Uraguai* describes only a portion of the campaign of 1756; under the leadership of the poem's ostensible hero, Gomes Freire de Andrade, Governor of Rio de Janeiro, the combined Portuguese and Spanish forces routed their enemy and occupied the mission settlements. In the culminating Battle of Caaibaté (10 February 1756), approximately 1,500 Indians were killed, 154 captured; the Portuguese and Spanish suffered a total of 4 dead and 40 wounded. The battle lasted one hour and fifteen minutes.[8]

Three years after the events described in Gama's poem, the Jesuits were expelled from Portugal and its colonies by the country's powerful prime minister, Pombal. Pope Clement XIV suppressed the Society of Jesus in 1773; it did not reemerge until 1814. A discussion of the Jesuit question, one of the major ideological struggles of the eighteenth century, is impossible here; yet a brief examination of the Society's presence in the region will clarify the historical and intellectual background of *O Uraguai.*

Around 1685 the Society of Jesus had begun to establish settlements known as the missions, or reductions, of Paraguay in the no-man's-land separating Portuguese and Spanish America. The missions were concentrated in the valleys of the Paraná and Uruguay rivers, in what is now southern Paraguay and northwestern Argentina (provinces of Misiones and Corrientes); only the seven towns that would play a role in the war of 1754-1759 lay on the eastern bank of the Uruguay, today southern Brazil. The Jesuits catechized the Tupi-Guarani peoples; their churches and religious houses formed the nucleus of each town. They learned the languages of their charges, taught

---

[8]These figures are from the "Diário da Expedição de Gomes Freire," published in the *Revista do Instituto Histórico e Geográfico Brasileiro* 16 (1853): 139-328.

them to read, composed grammars and vocabularies, translated religious texts. They administered the economy, which was based on livestock and the cultivation of maize, sweet potatoes, tobacco, maté, and cotton. Harvested crops and manufactured products were stored in public warehouses and distributed by the padres, who also decided all civil and criminal cases without appeal to the ordinary Spanish tribunals. White colonizers were discouraged from settling in the region. Thus the missions grew increasingly less dependent on the colonial government. The friends of the Society of Jesus believed the settlements embodied the primitive Christian ideal of communism, a "society presided over by Saint Paul, and the establishment of which Fourier, Robert Owen... and a host of others have attempted to revive in our day."[9] In contrast, the enemies of the Society believed that the Jesuit missions represented an empire within an empire, a "sterile, theocratic despotism" that had no place in the modern world.[10] In general terms, this was the stance taken by both José Basílio da Gama and Richard Burton. Among many other things, O Uraguai is an anti-Jesuit poem; its author showed as much enmity for the missionaries as he did sympathy for their Indian flock. The Jesuit matter is merely a symbol for a complex set of attitudes involving Old World and New, European and Indian, culture and nature, religion and progress, past and present.

THE POET

Sir Richard Burton's "Biographical Notice of the Life and Writings of José Basílio da Gama" contains most of the pertinent facts for an understanding of the poet and his work. With his customary enthusiasm, the translator had immersed himself in Gama's life as he would immerse himself in less delicate subjects while translating the Arabian Nights some fifteen years later. Burton seems to have been attracted to the Uraguai

[9]Burton, Letters from the Battle-fields, p. 32.
[10]Ibid., p. 27.

partly out of sympathy for its author's life. One could say of Sir Richard himself, as he said of the Brazilian, that "the spirit of Fortune . . . seemed to delight in driving him from place to place. As his youth was unhappy his age was miserable."[11] Born in the province of Minas Gerais, Gama would die at the age of fifty-four in Lisbon. Though still a teenager at the time of the war described in the *Uraguai*, he could not avoid hearing of the events and places of the conflict. His great-grandfather, Capt. Leonel da Gama Belles, had served in Colônia do Sacramento and had known José Fernandes Pinto Alpoim, brigadier general in the campaign against the Jesuit missions (*Uraguai*, I. 99-104). It is believed that Alpoim took charge of the young Basílio da Gama's education in Rio de Janeiro.

As was the violently anti-Jesuit Voltaire, Gama was educated by the Society of Jesus, from approximately 1754 until its expulsion from Brazil five years later. He would continue his studies in Rome, where he was apparently admitted to the Jesuit seminary. Recent scholarship has uncovered some facts, unknown to Burton, regarding this period. Gama, in his early twenties and a foreigner with no published works to his credit, was chosen a member of the prestigious Arcadia Romana. It is now clear that the future poet owed this honor to the influence of one or more of his Jesuit mentors. The closing lines of *O Uraguai* (V. 145-146) allude to a "Mireo" in Arcady: an anagram of the Jesuit Michele Giuseppe Morei's surname. The lines are an expression of gratitude rendered to a former teacher by Gama, whose poem was now worthy of entering the Arcadian groves on its own merit.[12]

[11]MS, fol. 89.

[12]See Antônio Cândido, *Vários Escritos* (São Paulo: Duas Cidades, 1970), pp. 164-165. For additional information on the same personality and his relationship with the poet, see Mário Camarinha da Silva's edition of *O Uraguai* (Rio de Janeiro: AGIR, 1964), p. 98n; Wilson Martins, *História da Inteligência Brasileira*, 2 vols. (São Paulo: Cultrix, 1977-1979), 1: 427. At first Burton believed *Mireo* to be Gama's "poetical, or pastoral name" (*The Highlands of the Brazil* 1 [1869; rpt. New York: Greenwood Press, 1969], p. 144). But in the biographical sketch that accompanies the poem, he gives the correct name assumed by the poet in the Arcadia Romana, Termindo Sipílio. See also note to V.146.

As a result of his travels and readings, the Brazilian poet may have acquired some of the liberal ideas that were gaining currency in Europe during the last half of the eighteenth century, perhaps in spite of his Jesuit training. We might recall that Rousseau's *Discourse on the Origin and Bases of Inequality*, with its celebration of the "natural man," had appeared in 1754, precisely during the Jesuit war that Gama would describe fifteen years later in *O Uraguai*. The poet read Voltaire, whose *L'Ingénu* (1767) created a kind of noble savage among the Huron Indians of Canada, as Gama would do among the Tupi-Guaranis of South America, with the attendant criticism of religious hypocrisy.[13] It is difficult to ascertain whether Gama harbored any specifically anti-Jesuit feelings before the publication of *O Uraguai*. At any rate, he had shown no animosity toward the Society before he was arrested in 1769 and accused of being a Jesuit sympathizer. The punishment for such "enemies of the state" was severe: a term in prison or exile to Africa. Before the sentence could be carried out, Gama wrote an epithalamium in honor of the marquis of Pombal's daughter. This work praised the progressive measures of the prime minister of Portugal as well as the bride; the poet had now placed himself squarely against his Jesuit past. Pombal, "a truer Maecenas than Richelieu," saved Gama from banishment to Angola.[14] Without wasting time, the poet published *O Uraguai*, whose text was probably almost complete. In the short time that elapsed between the printing of the *Epitalâmio* and the completion of *O Uraguai*, Gama must have added his anti-Jesuit notes. The poem justified Pombal's campaign against the Jesuits while glorifying Portuguese exploits in South America.

---

[13]There may be echoes of Voltaire's *Alzire* in Gama's "Peruvian" sonnet about Tupac Amaru, and the Brazilian poet also translated Voltaire's tragedy *Mahomet*. Cacambo, one of Gama's Indian heroes in *O Uraguai*, has the same name as the French writer's character in *Candide*, but if this may be related to some influence, it is equally likely that both authors were using the name of a real Indian. The similarity between the two characters does not go beyond the identical name. See Frederick C. H. Garcia, "Richard Francis Burton and Basílio da Gama: The Translator and the Poet," *Luso-Brazilian Review* 12, 1 (Summer 1975): 37-38 and n. 15, p. 55.

[14]Burton, "Biographical Notice," MS, fol. 85.

O Uraguai also lauds another of the prime minister's actions: the spectacular rebuilding of Lisbon after the earthquake of 1755 (III. 234-254).

If the epithalamium had saved Gama from exile, *O Uraguai* earned him letters of nobility and an appointment in the Ministry of Foreign Affairs. He spent the remainder of his life in the relative security of a government post. In his "Biographical Notice," Burton probably exaggerates the degree to which the poet suffered after the demise of Pombal in 1777. As in other works, Sir Richard seems to be projecting his own virtues here: more than Gama, he had learned the "sad penalty of telling truth" from years of service in the Foreign Office.[15] As Basílio had followed the winds of change with regard to the Jesuit question, so he managed to stay in favor with the reactionary government of Maria I after the marquis's fall from power. In the first year of her reign, he wrote a sonnet acclaiming the new queen. Ten years later Gama was made "Cavalier to the Queen" as a reward for thirteen years of loyal service under both regimes. Finally, he received the decoration of Saint James with a handsome perpetual income.

In addition to ill health, at least two events probably embittered Gama's later years. In 1786 the Jesuit Lorenz Kaulen published his vindictive *Resposta Apologética*, a three-hundred page book which answered all of the charges that were made against the Society in the text and in the notes of *O Uraguai*.[16] The tract also attempted to show the author as a man of evil character and meager literary talent. Finally, a few months before Gama's death in 1795, he was belatedly elected to the Royal Academy of Sciences in Lisbon as a mere corresponding member. This must have been a disappointment, for Gama's work shines in comparison with that of the academy's full members, most of whom have been consigned to literary oblivion.

[15]Ibid., MS, fol. 89.

[16]The full title of the work is *Reposta* [sic] *Apologética ao Poema Intitulado "O Uraguai," Composto por José Basílio da Gama e Dedicado a Francisco Xavier de Mendonça Furtado, Irmão de Sebastião José de Carvalho, Conde de Oeiras e Marquês de Pombal* (Lugano: n.p., 1786). See Bibliography.

THE POEM

It is not easy to define *O Uraguai*. In the first place, the poet had some epic intention. For Basílio da Gama, a son of the Enlightenment with its neoclassical norms, the epic represented the summit of the poetic hierarchy. In Brazil and Portugal most poets still labored under the shadow of Camoens, even if they could not find a theme as spectacular as Vasco da Gama's voyage to India. The colonial writers futilely sought for historical deeds that would justify the creation of an epic poem, which might then elevate Brazil to the heights reached by the mother country in *Os Lusíadas*. The early colonization depicted in José de Santa Rita Durão's *Caramuru* (1781) and the efforts of the settlers in the mining region portrayed in Cláudio Manuel da Costa's *Vila Rica* (1773), for example, did not possess enough vigor to generate an epic. Nor, for that matter, did the unequal, miserable, and brutal Guaranitic war chosen by Basílio da Gama. Such minor and recent historical events were hardly compatible with a poetic narration in which the heroic joined with the marvelous, according to the classical definition. Yet Gama somehow managed to transcend the limits of his materials and to project his poem onto a symbolic and national plane in the epic tradition: *O Uraguai* is the poem of encounter between European and American man.

Burton described the Brazilian's poem as a romance in verse; he was closer to a workable definition than most readers of the time, who thought of *O Uraguai* as a modern epic. One twentieth-century critic, discussing the theme of primitivism versus the organized world of the Europeans, believes the poem could be called a romance of exotic adventures.[17] We may never have an entirely accurate definition of the work, since it stubbornly and delightfully resists critical classification.

Burton seemed to think that the most heroic aspect of *O Uraguai* was not the action of its plot but rather Basílio da Gama's determination to avoid echoes of previous epic poems.

---

[17]Cândido, *Vários Escritos*, p. 175.

"He despised the pen worn subjects of remote antiquity . . . the Trojan clique, the . . . exhausted subjects of Portuguese discovery and the romantic tales made their own by Ariosto and Tasso."[18] Gama exiled the gods and other mythological machinery from his poem. The supernatural is reduced to a prophetic vision granted Lindóia by the tribal witch, and a brief personification of the river Uruguay—a kind of benign native spirit who intervenes to help the Indian warrior Cacambo reach the enemy camp:

Já sabia entanto
A nova empresa na limosa gruta
O pátrio rio; e dando um jeito à urna
Fez que as águas corressem mais serenas.

Saw the new emprize
Far in his silty grot the patrial Stream
And with propitious gesture tilts his urn
To will its liquid crystal kindly smooth.

[III. 92-95][19]

Gama also broke with tradition in the form he chose for his poem: ten-syllable blank verse with no strophic divisions; five cantos instead of the hallowed ten, twelve, or more. With its clear action leading from conflict to denouement, its adherence to the so-called Aristotelian unities, and the utter defeat of the Indians, O Uraguai in fact evokes a classical tragedy with five acts.[20]

The eighteenth century's valuation of nature and reverence for the natural brought a desire to simplify the laws of artistic composition. Just as Basílio da Gama removed rhyme

[18]Burton, "Notice of the Uruguay," MS, fol. 93.

[19]All quotations of O Uraguai, with modernized spelling, are from the princeps edition (Lisbon: Na Oficina de José da Silva Nazaré, 1769; rpt. Rio de Janeiro: Academia Brasileira de Letras, 1941). The latter is a commemorative edition, annotated by Afrânio Peixoto, Rodolfo Garcia, and Oswaldo Braga in honor of the poet's second centenary. Of course, all quotations of O Uraguai in English are from Sir Richard Burton's translation.

[20]Wilson Martins, História da Inteligência Brasileira, 1: 428-429.

and archaic rhetorical devices from his poetic language, so he achieved a new freedom of conception in the structure of *O Uraguai*: the poem resembles a linear chronicle more than it does the classical epic, which begins *in medias res*. The first two cantos of the poem are largely historical, introducing the principals and setting the scene for the action.[21] After the formulaic invocation and the dedication to Mendonça Furtado, brother of the marquis of Pombal, we see the Portuguese camp and a muster of the troops. During a banquet in his tent, the hero Andrade explains the causes of the war to a messenger from his Spanish ally. In an earlier campaign the Portuguese troops had been forced to bivouac in trees during the flooding of the Jacuí River; "perhaps a similar deed cannot be found in History," says Gama in a note to his poem.

As tendas levantei, primeiro aos troncos.
Depois aos altos ramos: pouco a pouco
Fomos tomar na região do vento
A habitacão aos leves passarinhos.

My tents in sylvan trunks at first I picht
Then on the lofty branches: step by step
High in the windy realm we clomb to seek
Houses and homes amid the buoyant birds.
[I. 217-220]

In the second canto the troops march and confront the enemy on an open plain. Andrade releases his Indian prisoners in an effort to find a peaceful solution. He then confers with two warriors, Cacambo and Sepé. Andrade presents the European case; the Indians, theirs and the Jesuits'. The Guaranis must give up their land, the general says,

Ao bem público cede o bem privado.
O sossego da Europa assim o pede.
Assim o manda o Rei.

[21]Ibid., 1: 430. The author's analysis of the *Uraguai*'s structure is excellent.

For private welfare bows to public weal.
The peace of Europe claims the Sacrifice
And thus the King commands.

[II. 137-139]

To this abstract political reasoning the Indians oppose a con-
crete personal argument: Since time immemorial they have in-
habited and worked this land where their ancestors are buried.
In four famous lines, Cacambo may invent the idea of America
for Americans—lines that would echo during the struggle
against colonial rule in the next century:

Gentes de Europa, nunca vos trouxera
O mar, e o vento a nós. Ah! não debalde
Estendeu entre nós a natureza
Todo esse plano espaço imenso de águas.

Ye sons of Europe, would that ne'er the wind
And wave had borne you hither! Not in vain
Nature between ourselves and you hath spread
The water-wilderness, this vasty deep.

[II. 171-174]

Perhaps in order to preclude any suspicion of antireligious
motives on the part of the European army, Gama has the Indi-
ans (and, by implication, the Jesuits) commit the crime of lese
majesty:

Vê que o nome dos Reis não nos assusta.
O teu está mui longe; e nós os Índios
Não temos outro Rei mais do que os Padres.

Thou seest the vain word "King" affrights us not.
Thine dwelleth far, afar; we Indian men
Own the good Fathers as our only Kings.

[II. 108-110]

The two irreconcilable sides must fight. The duel between the
Hispanic troops with their pistols and artillery and the Guaranis

with their spears, arrows, and breastplates of animal hide
embodies a contrast between technology and nature. The obvi-
ous result of such a disparate match is the slaughter of the Indi-
ans. Here Sepé dies at the hands of José Joaquín de Viana,
Spanish governor of Montevideo:

> *Não quis deixar o vencimento incerto*
> *Por mais tempo o Espanhol, e arrebatado*
> *Com a pistola lhe fez tiro aos peitos.*
> *Era pequeno o espaço, e fez o tiro*
> *No corpo desarmado estrago horrendo.*
> *Viam-se dentro pelas rotas costas*
> *Palpitar an entranhas...*

The Spanish Chieftain may no longer leave
Victory doubtful; fires his ready hand
Point-blank his pistol at the warman's breast.
Scant was the space between; the bullet dealt
To the nude frame a dreadful mortal wound.
Between the shattered ribs exposed appear
The palpitating vitals...

                              [II. 344-350]

If the first two cantos of *O Uraguai* could be called his-
torical, the third is symbolic, cornerstone of the entire poem.[22]
As the hero Andrade marches inexorably closer to the Guarani
settlements, Cacambo has his celebrated dream; the image of
the slain Sepé urges him to avenge their defeat by setting fire to
the Hispanic camp. In unforgettable lines we see the Indian
hero, assisted by the forces of nature, swim in darkness across
the river Uruguay to carry out his mission. As Cacambo
escapes, Gama tellingly compares him to Ulysses, and the fire
to the burning of Troy. Then,

> *De um alto precipício às negras ondas*
> *Outra vez se lançou, e foi de um salto*
> *Ao fundo rio a visitar a areia.*

---

[22]Ibid., 1: 429-430.

From the tall headland in the inky waves
Diving another time with downward plunge,
He sinks to seek the sands that floor the stream.
[III. 112-114]

When he returns home, the heroic Indian is poisoned by the
Jesuit Balda. Cacambo's murder may be a pretext for the most
celebrated episode in *O Uraguai,* the suicide of his bereaved
widow, Lindóia, in the following canto. Before her death, how-
ever, she has a vision, under the influence of the sorceress
Tanajura, in which the city of Lisbon is destroyed by the earth-
quake and reconstructed through the efforts of the great Pom-
bal. The prophetic vision seems arbitrary, a sop to Gama's
patron; yet symbolically, the earthquake and the rebuilding of
Lisbon foreshadow the destruction of the Jesuit villages and
their implicit reconstruction as part of Luso-Brazilian civi-
lization.[23]

The fourth canto fuses the historical and symbolic levels
of the poem. Andrade puts out the fire in his camp and finds
the village abandoned and burned by order of the Jesuits:

Tinham ardido as míseras choupanas
Dos pobres Índios, e no chão caídos
Fumegavam os nobres edifícios,
Deliciosa habitação dos Padres.

The flames devoured the wretched hovel-homes
Of the poor Redskins, and upon the ground
Smouldered and smoked each nobler edifice,
Delightful dwellings of the Reverend Men.
[IV. 265-268]

Meanwhile, Lindóia has sought out a lonely bower in the forest
for her suicide. She dies of a snakebite amid some of the most
delicate and sensual images in the poem:

Este lugar delicioso e triste,
Cansada de viver, tinha escolhido
Para morrer a mísera Lindóia.
Lá reclinada, como que dormia,
Na branda relva, e nas mimosas flores,
Tinha a face na mão, e a mão no tronco
De um fúnebre cipreste, que espalhava
Melancólica sombra. Mais de perto
Descobrem que se enrola no seu corpo
Verde serpente, e lhe passeia, e cinge
Pescoço, e braços, e lhe lambe o seio...
Inda conserva o pálido semblante
Um não sei quê de magoado e triste,
Que os corações mais duros enternece.
Tanto era bela no seu rosto a morte!

This spot most beautiful, most melancholy,
Had chosen weary of her wretched life
Hopeless Lindóia for her bed of death.
Reclined, as lulled in downy sleep, the Bride
Upon the verdant turf and varied flowers,
Hand-propped her cheek the while her arm was wound
Round the funereal Cypress glooming earth
With black lugubrious shades. A nearer view
Shows that around her body is enrolled
A green-hued serpent that now glides now coils
O'er neck and arms and licks her lovely breasts...
While still preserve her features wan and fixt
A something telling of a boundless woe,
A voiceless grief that melts the stoniest heart:
So beautiful upon her face was Death.
                              [IV. 149-159, 194-197]

The parallel deaths of Cacambo and Lindóia—man and woman, husband and wife—represent the end of the noblest Indians and foretell the demise of native culture.

The fifth canto of *O Uraguai* has been the most controversial ever since the poem's first reader, a royal censor, approved the work for publication: "The denouement does not seem natural to me," said João Pereira Ramos de Azevedo Coutinho in 1769. [24] If the previous four cantos function on a historical or symbolic plane, the last canto becomes allegorical and polemical. On the ceiling of the mission church, the victorious European troops see frescoes depicting the nefarious history of the Jesuits. It seems absurd that the members of the Society would have had themselves painted in such a negative light. Readers with an anti-Jesuit bias have tried to defend this section of O Uraguai. Burton was one of these readers: "The description of the tableaux found in the principal establishment of the Jesuits," he says, "leads to the artful enumeration of their deeds or rather their crimes and thus it is essentially useful to the end inculcated by the poem." [25] In this sense the fifth canto could have an ethical justification that is largely extrinsic to the poem. Aesthetically, the best way to justify these lines would be to consider them a kind of appendix, like Gama's vitriolic notes. The notes must be taken into consideration, but they can form an obstacle to an intrinsic, poetical reading of the text.

In spite of the poem's anti-Jesuit surface, the underlying theme of O Uraguai is the conflict between different cultures. This dialectic becomes evident when we recall that the work was first published in Lisbon by a man from Brazil, then was translated in Santos by a man from England. The opposition between Indian and European, nature and civilization, reveals itself in the structure of O Uraguai, in its imagery, and in Gama's use of counterpoint. [26] During the muster of troops on

[24]Quoted in José da Silva Bastos, História da Censura Intelectual em Portugal (Coimbra: Imprensa da Universidade, 1926), pp. 156-157.

[25]"Notice of the Uruguay," MS, fol. 96. Italics in MS. See below under the heading "The Manuscript and Two Mysteries." In his Preface, even Burton finds some incompatibility between the "harsh railings against the Societas Jesu" and the rest of the poem (fol. 1).

[26]Antônio Cândido, "O ritmo do mundo," Minas Gerais, Suplemento Literário (7 Sept. 1968), p. 4. The following analysis is based on the lines of Cândido's argument.

each side (Cantos I and IV), the Indian caciques parallel the
European gallery of heroes; the braves decked out in yellow and
blue feathers correspond to the infantry dressed in "azure white
and gold"; the red plumage of Sepé's warriors reflects the scar-
let uniform of the Portuguese grenadiers. In Canto III, the
shifts in point of view from Indian to European, Cacambo to
Andrade, seem almost cinematic. When the Jacuí River floods
its plain (Canto I), the troops pitch tents in trees and travel by
canoe; Gama compares the scene to Venice "in a stranger ele-
ment grown." Whatever his ostensible motivation for writing
O Uraguai, Basílio da Gama identified himself poetically with
his native America, the land and its inhabitants (the Indians;
sympathy with the Jesuits would have meant exile in Angola, or
worse). "Evidently not against his will," said Burton, "he be-
trays sympathy for the 'noble savage,' the victim of priestly
seduction."[27] In a contradiction typical of Enlightenment
thought, Gama exalted natural men while insisting on the need
to integrate them within the rational world of civilization.

Compared to the Guarani protagonists, the Portuguese
hero Andrade, irreproachable in his behavior, appears
strangely wooden: brave and even compassionate, yet in the
end a vehicle for the international policy of remote European
sovereigns. He lacks intimacy next to the Indians, especially
Cacambo and Lindóia, whom we perceive in their dreams and
visions as well as in their words and actions—waking and sleep-
ing, in their conscious and subconscious lives. They have the
presence of concrete individuals who transcend any stereotype
of the "noble savage." In contrast, we might ask ourselves after
reading the poem if General Andrade needs to sleep and
dream.

O Uraguai was one of the first Brazilian poems to use the
land of the New World as an integral part of its poetic expres-
sion. Yet names of specific places are rare in the poem; the
American landscape is evoked in a generic way. Even the great
river of the title may receive no more than an epithet, *O pátrio*

[27]"Notice of the *Uruguay,*" MS, fol. 92.

Rio ("the patrial Stream"). *O Uraguai* abounds with vague topographic evocations: "The rapid current of a giant stream," "a fresh and winding vale," "The graceful swelling hill." Detractors of the poem, such as the author of the *Resposta Apologética,* have attributed this vagueness to Gama's lack of familiarity with the region. The Jesuit Kaulen even asserts that the poet did not know the correct name of the river of the title, the Uruguay.[28] Such objections miss the point that Gama did not intend his work to be primarily informative; his method was to evoke the places and events of the story rather than merely to describe them. He transformed the exterior world of the South American landscape into an arbitrary poetic space composed of lines and colors, embodied in the four elements of earth, water, fire, and air.[29] More a lyrical than a narrative poet in spite of himself, Gama's verse moves in images—visual images in particular. We have only to read the opening lines of *O Uraguai* to confirm this: deserted plain, pools of blood, dead victims of the war, circling vultures. Basílio da Gama found a wealth of new forms in the indigenous world, which he fused into an original artistic vision, transcending the polemical aspects of his poem.

In the final lines of his work, the poet predicts: "Uruguay! Men shall read thee." He then imagines his personified poem strewing barbarous American flowers in the foreign groves of Arcady. Gama's prophecy was correct: his *Uraguai* has been published and read more than any contemporary poem in the Portuguese language. Readers have praised or condemned the work; few have remained indifferent to it. Beginning with Kaulen's *Resposta Apologética,* some critics have opposed the poem on ideological grounds. As late as 1940, Rodolfo Garcia treated Kaulen's book as a blessing against such an evil work as *O Uraguai.*[30] In the same year, Carlindo Lélis spoke of the *Resposta*

---

[28]*Resposta Apologética,* p. 52.

[29]Cândido, "O ritmo do mundo," p. 4.

[30]"Notas Complementares as Anotações do Poeta ao seu Poema," in *O Uraguai,* pp. 105-149 (see n. 19 for complete bibliographical reference). Garcia's notes and the entire commemorative edition of *O Uraguai* tend to be

as a scandalous book, "in which the person of Basílio da Gama is mercilessly maligned and in which, in a language without style, without logic, without grammar and without elegance the Jesuits are defended."[31] Garcia and Lélis were both celebrating the poet's bicentennial. Most Luso-Brazilian men of letters have praised *O Uraguai*. Some have lauded the work because of its ideological content. The literary historian Sílvio Romero placed *O Uraguai* side by side with *Caramuru* as a work that echoed a past "we regard with pride."[32] In the preface to his edition of 1895, Francisco Pacheco emphasized the poem's sociological aspects. Others have praised the work on aesthetic grounds. Almeida Garrett, Portugal's first romantic poet, summarized the work's virtues in this way: "Natural scenes painted very well, of great and lovely descriptive execution; pure utterances, without affectation; versus which are natural but not prosaic, and when necessary sublime but not gaudy..."[33] Writers of the nineteenth century considered Gama one of the creators of a national literature independent of Portugal's. Machado de Assis, a serious critic and creator in his own right, stressed Gama's importance as the founder of a literary tradition.[34] The poet Antonio Gonçalves Dias and the novelist José de Alencar (the latter translated by Burton) would convert the Brazilian Indian, whose prototype was Basílio's Cacambo, into a national

---

pro-Jesuitical. In his "Preliminary Notes," Afrânio Peixoto aptly described this volume as "criticism and commemoration" (p. xxxvii).

[31]"Basílio da Gama e *O Uraguai*," *Revista das Academias de Letras*, No. 26 (Oct. 1940), p. 142.

[32]*História da Literatura Brasileira*, 2 vols. (Rio de Janeiro: Garnier, 1902-1903), 1: 191.

[33]João Batista da Silva Leitão de Almeida Garrett, *Bosquejo da Poesia Portuguesa* (1826; rpt. in *Obras Completas*, Lisbon: Empresa da História de Portugal, 1904), p. 31. Garrett's own poem *Camões* (1825) was clearly influenced by *O Uraguai*; two of its supposedly revolutionary features were the use of ten-syllable blank verse and the absence of strophic divisions.

[34]"Literatura Brasileira: Instinto de Nacionalidade" (1872; rpt. in *Crítica Literária* [Rio de Janeiro: W. M. Jackson, 1946]), p. 134.

symbol and hero. Because of its place in Brazilian poetry and in the history of ideas, *O Uraguai* has maintained its currency in the twentieth century. Five editions have appeared since 1900, as each generation has come to terms with the poem's lyrical and historical significance.

THE TRANSLATOR

Sir Richard Burton and his wife, Isabel, considered their years in Brazil as a sort of necessary exile. He described Santos as "that Weston-super-mud of the Far West, peculiarly fatal to the genus European, species Consul..."[35] In order to escape from the heat and malaria of the port city, the Burtons set up house in São Paulo, about fifty miles to the west and high enough to have a more temperate climate. The devoutly Catholic Isabel remodeled an abandoned convent for living quarters, including a forty-foot study for her husband. When he was not exploring the back country, there was little for Burton to do except write and consume large quantities of Brazilian *cachaça* or brandy. When this life became boring, the couple would attend parties in Rio or Petropolis, where the British consul was a celebrity in the culture-starved Brazilian society of the time. Even the emperor Dom Pedro II, reputedly called "a grandson of Marcus Aurelius" by Victor Hugo, showed admiration for the foreign visitor who had travelled so widely, who spoke so many languages, and who had already published more than a dozen volumes.

In addition to preparing official reports on geography and trade, Burton continued his prodigious literary work during the four years he spent in South America. He composed *The Highlands of the Brazil*, still the most informative memoirs of travel in the *sertão*.[36] *Letters from the Battle-fields of Paraguay*, an example of Burton's lively *rapportage*, was based on one of the cruelest wars in modern times: the combined forces

---

[35] *Letters from the Battle-fields*, p. 81.
[36] In 2 vols. (1869; rpt. New York: Greenwood Press, 1969).

of Brazil, Argentina, and Uruguay killed approximately
230,000 Paraguayan men. There was the promise of a book on
the Brazilian lowlands and the beginnings of a Tupi-Guarani
grammar; neither book was printed.[37] Burton also prepared
the introduction and notes to Albert Tootal's translation of
The Captivity of Hans Stade of Hesse, the autobiographical
tale of a man captured by cannibals in Brazil.[38] He wrote two
essays on ethnological matters,[39] and he translated three major
works of Brazilian literature: José de Alencar's *Iraçema or the
Honey-lips,* J. M. Pereira da Silva's *Manuel de Morais,* and
Basílio da Gama's *O Uraguai.*[40] Only the last remained unpub-
lished. Burton also worked on several other books, none of
which dealt with Brazilian subjects.

    The Highlands of the Brazil and *Letters from the Battle-
fields* give us clues to the British consul's personal life which will
help us to understand his translation of Gama's poem. In nei-
ther book did Burton attempt to curb his disdain for the Catho-
lic church and, in particular, for the Jesuits. He wrote that the
religious schools in Brazil were "fifty years behind the world,"
and that dispensations to commit incest could still be obtained
for a fee.[41] He blamed the backwardness of Paraguay on the
isolation imposed by the Jesuits before their expulsion in 1759.

[37]Burton talks about this book in *Letters from the Battle-fields,* p. 33. See also
Alfred Bates Richards, Andrew Wilson, and St. Clair Baddeley, *A Sketch of
the Career of Richard F. Burton* (London: Waterlow & Sons, 1886), p. 81.

[38]London: Hakluyt Society, 1874. This book is a cardinal example of Burton's
compulsive annotation; his 250 notes are longer than the narrative itself.

[39]"The Primordial Inhabitants of Minas Gerais, and the Occupations of the
Present Inhabitants," *Journal of the Royal Anthropological Institute* 2 (1873):
407-423; "Notes on the Kitchen-Middens of São Paulo, Brazil, and the
Footprints of St. Thomas, alias Zomé," *Anthropologia* 1 (1873): 44-58.

[40]*Iraçema* and *Manuel de Morais* were published later in one volume (London:
Bickers and Son, 1886). For complete titles, see Bibliography. The title page of
Iraçema gives Isabel Burton as the translator; *Manuel de Morais* is presented as
as a joint venture by husband and wife. Actually, both were translated by
Richard Burton alone, as was *The Uruguay,* in spite of Lady Burton's claims.
See Frederick C. H. Garcia, "Richard Francis Burton and Basílio da Gama,"
p. 36.

[41]*Highlands of Brazil* 1: 332, 397.

Visiting the devastated Asunción, he said the city possessed a thin varnish of civilization, but "the slightest scratch shows under the Paraguayan Republic the Jesuitized Guarani."[42] Lady Burton became so distressed by these anti-Catholic salvos that she attached a protest to *The Highlands* (without her husband's knowledge) warning the reader against the book's moral pitfalls.

In contrast to his wife, called "Isabel the Catholic" by one biographer, Burton had no religious convictions during this time of his life. With his wealth of experience among non-Christians in Asia and Africa, any attempt to impose Western religion and culture on other peoples grated on Sir Richard's sensibility. He believed that missionary work in India made bad Christians out of good Hindus and Moslems; nothing was more despicable to him than the African who had given up his own culture for a sham Christianity. Burton usually favored the Oriental over the Occidental, the native over the invader. His sympathy for the Indians and his odium for the Jesuits in Gama's *Uraguai* should not surprise us.

Lady Burton once astutely observed that she belonged to the Middle Ages and her husband to the twentieth century. Sir Richard may have wished to draw her away from Christianity as much as she wished to convert him to the faith; he rarely missed a chance to snipe at the Church or his wife's piety. During a holiday in Madeira in 1862, he wrote to a friend: "My wife is too frantic with running about the churches and chapels and convents and other places of idolatrous abominations to do anything else . . . her only danger was of being burned for a Saint." Burton even seemed to derive a kind of pleasure from the excitable Isabel's discomfort, whether in religion or everyday matters. Before one trip he wrote, "My wife is fretting herself into a fever which as you may imagine greatly adds to the pleasure of departure."[43]

---

[42]*Letters from the Battle-fields*, p. 444.

[43]Lord Houghton Papers, Trinity College Library, letters dated 17 February 1863, 29 March 1863, 23 August 1861.

The personal drama of the Burtons explains some of Sir Richard's motivation for rendering *O Uraguai* into English. If he chose the work partly to spite Lady Isabel, she may have had the last word after her husband's death, as we will see. At any rate, Burton's own ideas were consistent with Gama's progressive notions, anti-Jesuitism, and sympathy for the natives. The dialectic of "civilization" and "barbarism," Occident and Orient, lies at the heart of all the Englishman's work.[44] In addition, Burton believed that the British reading public would prefer "typical" works containing primitive, exotic elements, as did *O Uraguai* and the Brazilian novels he translated.[45] Finally, he chose to translate writers with whom he felt a special compatibility—Camoens, Catullus, the anonymous poets of the *Arabian Nights*. We have already seen how he may have misread some facts of Gama's career in order to achieve this urgent sense of identity, which one biographer describes as the "most arresting and significant aspect" of his life.[46] Burton had a need to relate his literary work to a vital, existential concern; he believed that he was reliving the events of Gama's poem one century later in the Paraguayan War.

The prose of Sir Richard's Preface and biographical and critical notices to *The Uruguay* is characteristically Burtonian —by turns robust, pedantic, quaint, argumentative, ironic, but always original and personal. His Preface attempts to place the War of the Seven Reductions in a historical perspective. Burton's major source was the *História Geral do Brasil* of Francisco Adolfo de Varnhagen, a man not known for his good will toward the Jesuits. Yet Sir Richard managed to be rather fair

---

[44]Burton dedicated his *Letters from the Battle-fields* to Domingo Faustino Sarmiento, president of Argentina and author of *Civilización y barbarie* (*Facundo*), the prototypic Latin American work on the conflict between the Europeanized classes of the city and the uneducated inhabitants of the hinterland.

[45] *Iraçema* deals with the tragic love of a Portuguese soldier and an Indian maiden; *Manuel de Morais* is a colonial tale of conflict between religious duty and profane love.

[46]Brodie, *The Devil Drives*, p. 337.

and businesslike in his discussion of the conflicts behind the events related in the poem. We do not always find him so objective and serene, as we can see by comparing these pages to his treatment of the Jesuit question in *Letters from the Battlefields,* or even in his appendixes to *The Uruguay.* Burton's critical notice ("Appreciation"), although redundant at times, summarizes the poem's primary historical and aesthetic values.

Sir Richard signed the Preface to *The Uruguay* with his pseudonym, Frank Baker. He had adapted this nom de plume from his own middle name and the maiden name of his mother; his original poems *Stone Talk* (1865) and *The Kasîdah of Hâjî Abdû El-Yezdî* (1880) were also published under the pseudonym. Why did Burton use it? He seemed to be more sensitive of his reputation as a poet than as a writer of prose. His intuition was probably correct; few readers would argue that Burton's original poetry and translations maintain the quality of his best prose.[47] While yearning to be recognized as a poet, Burton took pains to conceal what he considered the poetic or "feminine" aspects of his own personality.

THE TRANSLATION

The Uruguay stands both as a scrupulous rendition of Basílio da Gama's poem and as an independent creation in its own right. Burton's interest in exotic literature and peoples was an expression of the same impulse that sent him and other British explorers, such as Livingstone, Layard, and Speke, to unknown lands. Unlike most works of the Victorian period, however, Sir Richard's translation of *O Uraguai* shows a very "modern" sympathy toward native culture and a hostility toward imperial efforts to replace or destroy it. His seeking of the exotic and primitive in this and other works can be seen as a way of escaping the horrors of industrialized England, as the Pre-Raphaelites escaped through a return to fifteenth-century Italy, and

---

[47]But it should be remembered that portions of *The Arabian Nights* were written in *saj'a* (rhymed prose), "Englished" in poetic prose by Burton.

Edward Fitzgerald escaped through the cult of Omar Khay-
yam. Burton felt the same uneasiness about colonial injustice
abroad as the most sensitive writers and thinkers felt about
social inequality at home. Figures as diverse as Carlyle, Dis-
raeli, Dickens, Ruskin, Arnold, and William Morris revealed a
preoccupation with the extremes of wealth and poverty, the
persistence of class privilege, and the misery of the masses. In
spite of the stereotypes of smugness and complacency normally
used in descriptions of the period, the Victorians were their
own most acute critics. In his presentation and even in his
translation of the *Uraguai,* Burton demonstrated the same
capacity for criticism as did his leading contemporaries. His
rendition of the poem represents an original and characteristic
contribution to the best literature of the Victorian period.

In his Preface, Burton says he "endeavoured to engraft
upon an English style as many of the Basilian peculiarities as
possible." This general principle is responsible for many of the
good qualities of the translation, and for some of its defects.

Burton chose to turn Gama's decasyllabic *heróico* line
into English blank verse. The following examples, which can be
read as iambic pentameters, show the Portuguese meter with
major accents on the sixth and tenth syllables:

Uruguay's rugged bróod, and in its blóod.   [I. 8]

Nor thou all-valiant Cástro did prefér.   [I. 122]

On occasion Gama used a variation of this basic meter, the
decassílabo sáfico, with stresses on the fourth, eighth, and
tenth syllables. Here are two of Burton's pentameters that can
also be scanned in the Portuguese manner:

The wines of Eúrope in the gólden bówls.   [I. 139]

On antique hatreds and ill-fóunded féuds.   [II. 116]

He would use the same metrical adaptation in his version of
Camoens's *Lusíadas.*

Because of his sense of fidelity to the original, Burton translated *The Uruguay* line by line, with few exceptions. He believed this system would free him from the imputation of "translator-traitor." The result is a text that sounds and looks like the original, but that may not always seem natural. The same character of visual and sound copy, coupled with an archaic style, triggered unfavorable reviews of *The Lusiads,* yet Burton was closer to poetic success in the work by Basílio da Gama.

Sir Richard's compulsion to remain faithful to the original led him to the use of English cognates for Portuguese words, most of them Latinate. As a result, he often chose uncommon or anachronistic words. For example, he employed "margent" from Gama's *margem* (III. 98), where "edge" or "bank" would have been satisfactory in meaning, if not metrically. In an extended simile, he translates the word *ninho* ("nest") as "natal nide" (I. 17), indulging his taste for alliteration and choosing an adjective that fits the passage. The use of the Shakespearian "sans" as a translation of the Portuguese *sem* ("without") and of "in fine" for *enfim* ("finally") belong to the same tendency to "photograph" the text. [48] Burton's criterion of loyalty sometimes led him away from Gama's idiomatic tone, which was free of preciosity. For the reader who knows both languages, the Portuguese original has aged less than its English version, written a century later.

With all his desire to be faithful, Burton took occasional liberties. It may be a minor matter, as in the scene of Lindóia's death with the snake at her chest; the translator described "her lovely breasts" (IV. 159) in a kind of personal tribute to the

---

[48]A rendition identical to that of *ninho* appears in Burton's translation of *The Lusiads* (III. 34). In Camoens's poem, the word *ninho* is rendered variously as "lair" (III. 36), "nide" without an adjective (VII. 30), VIII. 3), and "nest" (I. 10, VII. 68, VIII. 71). These examples illustrate Burton's method of translation in *Os Lusíadas,* with occasional use of uncommon words. His treatment of Gama's poem is similar. Other examples: I. 1, 9, 102, 128, 174, 177; II. 2, 19, 203, 258, 268, 323, 353; III. 14, 47, 50, 79, 133, 138, 232, 314; IV. 10, 30, 50, 58, 144, 166; V. 91, 104.

indigenous heroine. Some adjustments are metrical fillers, but Burton made more significant changes, too. In the muster of native troops, Gama says that the Indian warriors "consider it an insult to die of old age":

E que têm por injúria morrer velhos.

Captain Burton tells us that the braves

> most disdain
> To die of years, the soldier's deepest shame.
>
> [IV. 81-82]

Of course the shame only applied to soldiers on active duty; as a retired officer Sir Richard was entitled to live to a ripe age.[49]

Burton's mind teemed with Anglo-Saxon and Old English verse from his encyclopedic reading; this may have given him a fondness for alliteration. Sometimes the device is effective, as in this picture of the corpulent Jesuit Patusca, a sort of clerical Falstaff:

> Brother Patusca, bearing keys in belt,
> By weight of vastest paunch to earth attached.
>
> [IV. 115-116]

At other times, alliteration evokes a Nordic saga or an Old English epic more than it does a Brazilian poem:

> Now with a sheaf of shafts anew supplied
> He hies once more to fight anew the fight.
>
> [II. 317-318]

On one occasion, Burton has Cacambo and Sepé dress in a hybrid Scots-Guarani costume of kilts made from feathers

---

[49]Other examples of liberties taken by the translator can be found in I. 82; II. 242; III. 101; IV. 183, 214; V. 31.

(II. 43). Yet this is no more incongruous than Gama's comparing the Luso-Spanish attack against the Indians to an avalanche in the Alps (II. 293-298). In spite of his mastery of the Portuguese language, Sir Richard seems to have missed the sense of the original in at least one passage (II. 201-204). On the other hand, the translator may improve the princeps. Gama's description of the Indians' cavalry has been praised by critics, but Burton's rendering could be more effective, with its balance and onomatopoeia:

> *Tropel confuso de cavaleria:*

> A jostling troop of savage chivalry.   [IV. 106]

Finally, the most curious license taken by Burton, within his general fidelity to the text, is an intensification of pejorative lines referring to the Jesuits. This usually takes the form of an insertion of virulent adjectives. After the battle of Canto II, for example, General Andrade pities the corpses of the dead Indians, literally "victims of the (Jesuits') ambition for an unjust empire":

> *Vítimas da ambição de injusto império.*

Burton translates:

> *Butcher'd* ambitious lawless rule to build.   [III. 10]

When the Jesuits are expelled in Lindóia's prophetic vision, Gama hopes that the society's pupils (*alunos*) will have to wander across the seas. Burton inserts a characteristic adjective:

> may thy *hateful* brood
> Wander the waste of waters o'er.
>
>   [III. 284-285]

In similar instances, the blood spilled by Jesuit murders becomes a "*traitorous* stain" (III. 300), and the painted throne symbolizing the Society's power is transformed into a "*foul* throne" (V. 20). Surely such insertions cannot be explained away as metrical padding. Even in a prose passage like the argument of Canto V (translated from Varnhagen's edition), Burton adds another pejorative word: "general submission of the *misguided* Indians." The reader might think that Basílio da Gama's poem contains more than enough invective in the original without the addition of these Burtonian potshots. We may never know exactly why Sir Richard felt the need to exacerbate the anti-Jesuit character of *O Uraguai,* but the story of his manuscript's fate will give us some ideas.

THE MANUSCRIPT AND TWO MYSTERIES

There are several problems related to the manuscript of Burton's *Uruguay.* We can establish its dates within reasonable limits, but two unanswered questions remain: Why have the notes to the text disappeared, and why was the poem not published in Burton's lifetime?

A cloud of rumors and misinformation has surrounded the unpublished manuscript for the last hundred years. Most of Burton's biographers have repeated a litany of errors, beginning in his own lifetime when Richards, Wilson, and Baddeley described *The Uruguay* as an anthology of "translations from the great Brazilian authors."[50] The situation has been a little better in Brazil, but the critic Sacramento Blake created a long-lived misconception in 1898, when he affirmed that the text had been printed. In the Brazilian Academy's commemorative edition on the occasion of Gama's bicentennial, Oswaldo

---

[50]*A Sketch of the Career of Richard F. Burton,* p. 21. The same defective information appears in Francis Hitchman, *Richard F. Burton: His Early Private and Public Life With an Account of His Travels and Explorations,* 2 vols. (London: Sampson Low, Marston, Searle and Rivington, 1887) 2: 444; and in the biography by Burton's niece, Georgiana M. Stisted, *The True Life of Captain Sir Richard F. Burton* (London: H. S. Nichols, 1896), pp. 418-419. Some modern biographers have been more careful: Fawn Brodie, *The Devil Drives,* p. 242n; and Byron Farwell, *Burton* (New York: Holt, Rinehart and Winston, 1963), p. 409.

Braga corrected this notion: "Famous translation by Burton, quoted by Gama bibliographers who state that it has been published, but it was never printed."[51] It may surprise readers to see that the translation is called *famous* in the same sentence that declares it had never been published.

We have several hints to aid us in dating Burton's *Uruguay*. At the end of his critical notice to the poem, he signed "Santos April 23, 1867."[52] Lady Burton had some version of the poem with her, along with several other fruits of her husband's labor, when she embarked for England on 24 July 1868; her job was to find a publisher for these works in London.[53] When *Highlands of the Brazil* appeared the following year, we find a quotation of the final lines of *O Uraguai,* with some variants in comparison with the version published here. After Burton left Brazil in 1872, he stated in a letter to *The Athenaeum* that his translation was ready.[54] Yet some references in the manuscript indicate that the Preface was written (or at least revised) several years later. The key chronological allusion is to "the late M. de Varnhagen," the Brazilian historian and editor of *O Uraguai,* who died on 26 June 1878. In conclusion, then, we know that Burton worked on Gama's poem during his stay in Brazil, most likely in early 1867; the probable completion date of the first draft would be 23 April of that year, recorded at the end of the manuscript. By the time of the *Athenaeum* article (1872), the translation may have been ready for the press. But Burton did not put his final touches on the Preface, signed with the pseudonym Frank Baker, until some time after 1878, the year of Varn-

[51] Augusto Vitorino Alves Sacramento Blake, *Dicionário Bibliográfico Brasileiro* (Rio de Janeiro: Tipografia Nacional, 1898) 4: 330-334; *O Uraguai* (1941), p. 171.

[52] MS, fol. 97. In her biography of Burton, Lady Burton suggests he was working on the translation between February and the spring of 1867. *The Life of Captain Sir Richard F. Burton,* 2 vols. (1893; rpt. Boston: Milford House, 1973) 1: 436.

[53] *The Life* 1: 453-454; Brodie, *The Devil Drives,* p. 242.

[54] No. 2313 (24 February 1872), pp. 241-243.

hagen's death. Sir Richard's most dependable bibliographer, the devoted Norman M. Penzer, in fact dated the manuscript "at about 1878," without explanation.[55] We can be a little more specific than this; the second half of 1878 is the most probable date, for the reasons given above.

Penzer tells us that the manuscript had 155 sheets. This "Historical Romance of South America" or "epic poem," as he calls it, was "translated metrically (from the Portuguese) by Sir Richard Burton.... With notes, a biographical and critical notice of the author and an epilogue." There are some apparent discrepancies between Penzer's entry and the manuscript of *The Uruguay,* now in the Huntington Library, San Marino, California, used in preparing this edition. No portion of our document carries the rubric of "epilogue," but Burton's "Notice" or "Appreciation" of the poem, at the end of the manuscript, can be reconciled with Penzer's description. A more serious problem has to do with the total number of pages and the notes. The Huntington manuscript totals only 98 leaves (compared with Penzer's 155); it contains no notes to the text of the poem. In his late Preface, Burton himself referred to "copious notes for the student's use." His translation in fact has superscript numbers in 125 places, including the passages annotated in the standard editions of *O Uraguai* known to him (the princeps of 1769 and the Paula Brito edition of 1855; see Bibliography). All these facts, combined with Sir Richard's reputation as an irrepressible annotator, leave no doubt that the manuscript did contain notes at one time. What happened to them?

First of all, we should remember that José Basílio da Gama's notes to his own *Uraguai* (88) are much more anti-Jesuitic and polemical than the verse itself. Traditionally, they have been published with the poem; it seems unlikely that Burton, who was both pedantic and anti-Jesuitical, would have omitted these venomous barbs of the poet. The remaining notes (37) would have been Sir Richard's own voice in this complex counterpoint. We can imagine him waxing eloquent in notes on some of his favorite subjects, such as warfare, exotic flora and fauna, primitive ethnology, and the search for the sources of the Nile.[56] We can just as easily imagine him adding other notes detrimental to the Society of Jesus, perhaps based on his long experience in Portuguese Asia and Africa.

If Lady Isabel Burton had not burned and mutilated large portions of her husband's unpublished work after his death, we would not have the right to suspect her hand in the disappearance of the notes to *The Uruguay*. This book would have offended her Catholic sentiments more than any other work in the Burtonian canon. If the notes could be burned, all the overt charges against the church would go up in smoke. Some of the most bitterly anti-Jesuit sections of the manuscript reveal signs of tampering, if not of mutilation. In Burton's biographical notice, a passage referring to the "diabolical" precepts and actions of the society shows several words that are crossed out; another sentence has the word *crimes* (of the Jesuits) underlined.[57] If Lady Burton did tamper with the text and burn the notes, then why did she not destroy the verses of the poem itself? Perhaps she realized how much her husband loved the poem; he had worked on it over a period of ten years. Whatever her motives, we should be grateful that the verse was spared from this hypothetical auto-da-fé.

Lady Burton could have destroyed the notes during the six years by which she outlived her husband (1890-1896). Or the notes might have been victims of the second burning of manuscripts by her sister, Mrs. Fitzgerald, after Lady Burton's death. We will probably never know for certain. To complicate matters, Norman Penzer's description of *The Uruguay*, in his *Annotated Bibliography* of 1923, refers to all 155 folios and the

---

[56]V. 31-33. See Frederick C. H. Garcia, "Richard Francis Burton and Basílio da Gama," pp. 49-52.

[57]MS, fols. 90, 96.

notes. Perhaps his entry was based on the memory or annotations of two friends of his who had known Burton and were familiar with the manuscripts: Daisy Letchford Nicastro and F. Grenfell Baker.[58]

The problem of the missing notes leads to a second mystery: Why was Burton's *Uruguay* not published in his lifetime? While still in Brazil, he thought about finding a sponsor who would take interest in the translation; he even scribbled a dedication to the Honorable Manuel Pinto de Sousa Dantas, minister of agriculture. Unfortunately, the ministry had no funds earmarked for the publication of Brazilian works in English. Nor did the British government, as Burton complained in his letter to *The Athenaeum*. The genre of the *Uruguay* may have militated against its acceptance by a publisher in London: even in those more humanistic days, poetry did not have as large a readership as prose. "I found no market for the Brazilian translations," Isabel would say, "though I published two of them."[59] Sir Richard had been able to sell other books of verse. Did the publishers fail to understand the poem? Almost as if attempting

---

[58]Mme. Nicastro was living with the Burtons in Trieste at the time of Sir Richard's death. She would reproach Lady Burton for burning her husband's translation of the Arabic erotic classic, *The Scented Garden;* she wrote letters to Penzer relating "her surreptitious reading of many of the MSS. before they were burned, and the gems she found among them" (*An Annotated Bibliography,* p. 181). Dr. Baker was Burton's traveling physician; he attended Sir Richard at his deathbed. Like Daisy Letchford Nicastro, he condemned Lady Burton for the "ruthless holocaust" and was familiar with some of the writer's work in manuscript (*An Annotated Bibliography,* pp. x, 176). Yet there is still another proviso: in his catalog of Burton's works, Penzer says that *The Uruguay* "is now in the possession of a London bookseller" (p. 184). Presumably, the manuscript would have been available for his perusal. The Huntington Library's MS 27954 was purchased from the London firm of J. Pearson & Co., listed as item no. 315 in a catalog, entitled "Spain," and without date (letter by Tyrus Harmsen, former cataloguer at the Huntington, dated 5 November 1958). David Mike Hamilton, assistant curator of literary manuscripts, believes we can "say with reasonable certainty that the manuscript was purchased before 1925, when the Library began compiling records" (letter dated 7 February 1979). The London firm of J. Pearson & Co. is no longer in existence.

[59]*The Life* 1: 455.

to make *The Uruguay* more attractive to the layman, Burton
had invented a subtitle, *Romance of South America*. We might
speculate that Sir Richard had a system of priorities that placed
other works ahead of Gama's poem for publication; yet Bur-
ton's high opinion of *O Uraguai,* expressed in the manuscript
and elsewhere, discourages this line of reasoning.[60]

Part of the blame may rest on the shoulders of Sir Richard
himself. The translation did have some clear defects, above all
its archaic vocabulary and extremely idiosyncratic style. Bur-
ton was not present in London to submit the manuscript to an
editor with all the prestige and force of his own personality.
Here it would be possible to suspect Lady Burton once more,
since she customarily took care of her husband's publishing
needs while he traveled or filled his diplomatic posts. She would
obviously not be ebullient about the printing of a work that was
most offensive to her religious feelings. This may be one reason
for the survival of the text but not of the more overtly vitriolic
notes: Why destroy a poem her husband loved if she, his lit-
erary executrix, was making no effort to have it published any-
way? We may have a new form of censorship here, more subtle
than a holocaust and more effective, because not provoking
cries of outrage: censorship by neglect.

THE PRESENT EDITION

The manuscript of Richard Burton's *Uruguay* belongs to the
Huntington Library, San Marino, California (HM 27954). It
consists of ninety-eight numbered folios: a preface (fols. 1-9);
the text of the poem, including Burton's synopses of each canto
(fols. 10-79);[61] drafts of a title page and dedication (fol. 80,
front and back);[62] a "Biographical Notice of the Life and Writ-

---

[60]*Highlands of the Brazil* 2: 143-144; *Letters from the Battle-fields,* p. 142.

[61]Translated directly from *Épicos Brasileiros,* Varnhagen's edition of
O Uraguai and *O Caramuru* (Lisbon: Imprensa Nacional, 1845). The original
synopses were by A. J. da Serra Gomes.

[62]Burton's title page reads: "The Uraguay / (A Romance of Jesuit American
Warfare) / By José Basílio da Gama / Translated in English blank verse / by /

ings of José Basílio da Gama" (fols. 81-91); and a "Notice of the *Uruguay*" (fols. 92-98). The Preface and text of the translation were probably recopied by Burton from his original draft; they contain few corrections and are reasonably legible. The reverse sides of the pages in these two parts of the manuscript have alternate renderings of some lines from the poem. On the other hand, the two "Notices" at the end of the manuscript must be a rough draft: they are in Burton's notoriously crabbed hand-writing, illegible in many places, with numerous marginal notes and abbreviations on both sides of the folios, which sug-gest a tentative version; the text has been crossed through with a vertical line on each page. Both the biographical notice and the critical notice have apparently been numbered by different hands (1-11, 1-7, respectively).

Our purpose in preparing this edition is to offer a coher-ent, readable text. In the Preface and translation of the poem, we have virtually reproduced Burton's manuscript verbatim, with a few minor changes to make the spelling modern and consistent. Sir Richard left the punctuation of the verse incom-plete; using the princeps of *O Uraguai* as well as the other edi-tions, we have added or modified punctuation only where abso-lutely necessary to an understanding of the literal meaning of the text. Where alternate translations of a line exist, we have chosen the version we considered better poetry or closer to the original; often the rejected translation is included in the foot-notes. For the supplementary biographical and critical sec-tions, we have despaired of reproducing the manuscript ver-batim, with its hundreds of corrections and marginal squiggles, some of which seem to be directed to the translator himself rather than to the public. Therefore, we have chosen to edit these sections with the purpose of offering a readable text. Bur-ton's translations of additional poems by Gama and others have

---

Richd F. Burton/ With a short Biographical Notice/ of the Author." The subtitle of the present edition (*A Historical Romance of South America*) derives from Penzer, *An Annotated Bibliography*, p. 184.

been omitted; the 1,377 lines of *The Uruguay* will give the reader a sufficient idea of the Brazilian muse. After the text and notes to Burton's translation, a facsimile copy of the original 1769 Portuguese edition has been included by permission of the New York Public Library.

Most of José Basílio da Gama's own voluminous notes have been translated into English. The editors have placed all notes, Gama's and their own, after the text; the poet's notes in particular can prevent an intrinsic reading of the verse. All places where Burton proposed to have notes are also indicated. With regard to the title, we have preferred the modern English *Uruguay* in place of Gama's spelling for the river and the region (*Uraguay,* modern Portuguese *Uraguai*). Both Portuguese proper nouns and Indian words follow current Brazilian orthography.

Sir Richard admitted that his translation of Camoens's *Lusiads* was perhaps "wood-work, not bronze, and far less that which outlasts bronze." He might have said the same of his translation of *The Uruguay.* "Even wood, however," Burton added, "has claims upon the sympathy and affection of the handler; and I end my work not without regret."[63]

---

[63]*Camoens: His Life and His Lusiadas* 2: 677.

To
H. E. the Counsellor M. P. de S. Dantas
Minis[ter] of Agriculture and Public Works
Brazil
This first attempt I respectfully offer to the literature of his
native land to whose cause he has been so fervent a votary
of progress[1]

---

[1]Manuel Pinto de Sousa Dantas (1831-1894) had a long career as a member of
Parliament, minister in several cabinets, and prime minister. History has
confirmed that Burton's dedication did not contain empty praise: Dantas
would play an important role in the movement to abolish slavery in Brazil,
which was finally accomplished in 1888.

PREFACE
[Burton]

I cannot and I will not follow the beaten path of the normal translator—open proceedings with a "Short Life of the Poet"; proceed to an "Account of the Versions and the Editions which have hitherto appeared" and end with reasons why the present rendering should bear away the bell. Firstly the *Uraguai* has never been English'd; secondly I agree with the late Viscount de Varnhagen[1] that [it] is advisable to alter the order of an author whose Poem is at least as interesting as the Poet.

The Martial Music of the trumpet which proclaims the Conquest of Uruguay-land and the triumph of Liberty and Civilisation over barbarism and theocratic tyranny should not mingle with those harsh railings against the Societas Jesu, with that adulation of the Pombal family which ruled if it did not reign in Portugal, and with those dissertations on Tupi or South American words such as *Mate, Embira, Jacaré* and *Mandioca* which, though necessarily used in describing the life of Tupiland should, in the artist's hand, explain themselves. Truly offensive must be the hermeneutic farrago, with its "smell of oil," to those who would enjoy the delicate aroma of the poetic posy.

Let us, then, begin with the text of the favourite Brazilian Romantic epic or rather epical Romance, follow with copious notes for the student's use derived from a variety of authors and end with a biography of the Poet.[2]

But I find it necessary to prefix a few words concerning the subject of the *Uruguay*.

On Jan[uary] 16, 1750 the crowns of Spain and Portugal ratified in the best of faith the famous "Treaty of Limits"

(Canto I) which led unwittingly to the "War of the Seven Reductions," or Missions, a campaign of the Luso-Brazilians against the Hispano-Americans. By virtue of this instrument H[is] C[atholic] Majesty D. Ferdinando VI obtained exclusive jurisdiction over the Nova Colônia de Sacramento[3] in the Uruguay River, and H[is] M[ost] Faithful Majesty D. João V received in lien and incorporated with Brazil, the Jesuit Missionary stations or, as they were then called the "Reductions" (Canto I). This convention intended to prevent disorders and bloodshed led directly to the war which forms the praxis of the Poem.

While granting to Portugal the Jesuit establishments on the left or Eastern bank of the great River Uruguay,[4] now watering the Banda Oriental province in the Republic of Montevideo, the "Treaty of Limits" allowed the Tupi-Guarani catechumens virtually to be banished the Country and be transported to the lands lying South of the Ibicuí stream. The Fathers of the Company naturally complained that their dearest interests were thus deeply injured. They protested long and loudly against this injustice, transmitting through the Governor of Buenos Aires their memorials to the Royal Audiencies of Charcas and Lima and eventually to the Crown. Their Provincial assembled the Senior Missioners who pronounced the measure impracticable and the Superior travelled in person through the Reductions to prospect, it is supposed, their powers of resistance.

The Fathers, who were mostly foreigners, English, French and German, contemplated with terror forfeiting the vast regions of fertile soil, salubrious climate and majestic rivers, moated by the immensity of wild and wold that separated them from the sea and isolated them from all European establishments. This forfeiture they saw as the first step towards dispersing and secularizing their flocks of Red-skin followers, catechised by their zeal, energy and industry, disciplined and moralised by their example and counsels, and trained to toil in the laborious vineyard of the Lord and His Elect. They expected the worst from the Portuguese whom they hated and feared on account of the animus displayed against them by the great Minister Pombal and from the Luso-Brazilians, who not only drove them out of La Guaira, but also continually harried and harassed them in their own homes. It is needless to say more on this disputed question. Charlevoix[5] represents the Loyolist side in recounting the injuries. Southey and a host of Brazilian writers on the other hand who were hostile to the "Black Pope," declare that the *Bandeiras* (Razzias or Commandos) levied and conducted by the gallant "Mamelucos" or half-caste Indians of São Paulo, only hurled back Jesuitic encroachments upon Brazilian ground.

The thirty thousand Catechumens,[6] it is said, unanimously took part with their Pastors. They preferred the ultima ratio of the sword to going forth, like the children of Israel, into the Great Desert; they fought with extraordinary energy and they murdered with the accustomed savage alacrity. Their plans and strategy were reported, truly or falsely, to betray the direct inspiration of Europeans and something more than the barbarian's usual powers of imitation. The Jesuits, whose influence was then everywhere on the wane, fell under the suspicion of levying war against a friendly nation while loudly proclaiming themselves loyal and innocent men. Into this question, also, I have no intention of entering. The quarrel is between the Poet and the Jesuits.

When the Tupis formally rejected peace, the field was taken against them by the hero of the Poem, the Viceroy Gomes Freire de Andrade, created in 1758 Count of Bobadela,[7] a Portuguese of high family and of the right heroic stamp, one of the noblest spirits of his nation. The time occupied is a "unity" of about six months beginning on Jan[uary] 17, 1756 with the Review upon the "Campo das Mercês" (Canto I) and ending (Canto V) with the pacification of the Reductions in July of the same year. Their subsequent history offers no interest. Under Spanish governors and Franciscan monks the handwork of the Jesuits soon melted away; and in 1817 the Luso-Brazilians of Rio Grande do Sul completed the work of destruction. The actual state of their ruined settlements is well described by the late M. de Moussy.[8]

The subject has a higher interest than any colonial campaign however eventful. It was the first blow struck at the "Indian" empire of the mighty "Company" and its effect proved that the Colossus was not invulnerable. The five years' war of 1865-70 between Brazil and Paraguay was a mere repetition of History. The late Marshal-President López[9] never abandoned his Country's claim to the Sierra de las Misiones and to the Eastern tracts of the Corrientes Province. Hence José Basílio da Gama is still read in Brazil whither the Jesuits are slowly but surely returning.

In the humble part of a metrical translator my object has not been to trim between the "twin incompatibilities" — the literal and the license called liberty. It has been my aim throughout to produce the closest copy of my author, with a minimum repaid for the venerable Horatian precept:

Nec verbo verbum curabis reddere fidus.[10]

Wherever a version of so tight a fit does not offend sound or sense, many lines have been rendered word for word. I have studiously avoided the imputation of "translator = traitor." Even in the boldest recitativo the least ornamentation that wars against the characteristic simplicity has been rejected despite all temptation. I have endeavoured to engraft upon an English style as many of the Basilian peculiarities as possible. A translator longs to get rid of such cacophonies as Caitutu, Tatu-guaçu, Sepé and the truly dreadful "Cacambo." But they are necessities and, as such they must be accepted by the brave in letters.

I will conclude this preamble with the wise words of Victor Hugo, no mean judge in such matters: "To translate a foreign poet is to enrich the national literature."

FRANK BAKER[11]

At specus, et Caci detecta apparuit ingens
Regia, et umbrosae penitus patuere cavernae.[1]

Virgil, *Aeneid*, Lib. VIII

To His Excellency the Count of Oeiras

SONNET[2]

Build a bright and voluminous globe of jasper
And crown it with the statue of a perfect Hero;
But do not inscribe his name upon a narrow field,
For his name fills the earth and the deep sea.

Engrave upon the jasper, eloquent Artificer,
In a silent story many an illustrious deed:
Peace, Justice, Abundance and a constant heart;
This suffices us and our World.

But considering that in a future time
A Pilgrim born in places across the sea
May wonder who gives life to the lifeless jasper,

Show him also Lisbon rich and vast,
And her Commerce, and in a place remote and dark,
Hypocrisy weeping. This will suffice him.

... saevis ... periclis
servati facimus.[3]

Virgil, *Aeneid*, Lib. VIII

[1]The two Latin quotes not transcribed in Burton; also omitted in Varnhagen's *Épicos Brasileiros*. The first quote (VIII. 241-242) can be translated as: "Then Cacus's cave and enormous dwelling place (appeared), and the dark caverns became completely open."

[2]Not in Burton; also omitted in Varnhagen's edition.

[3]The passage is incomplete; in its entirety it is "... *saevis, hospes Troiane, periclis / servati facimus meritosque novamus honores*" (VIII. 188-198). Literally: "... saved from terrible dangers, O Trojan guest, we render and repeat these deserved honors."

45

CANTO I

ARGUMENT

Invocation — Dedication to Francisco Xavier de Mendonça Furtado, Captain-General of the Maranhão Province and brother of the Marquês de Pombal — Arrival in Camp of Catáneo the Spanish Messenger, with promises of aid — Review of the Troops — Banquet given by the Hero of the Poem, Gomes Freire de Andrade — Causes of the Campaign and how it opened.

Canto I

Still reek outstretching o'er the desert strands
Lakes of man's life-tide tepid and impure
Where float the fragments of the unsheeted dead
Baiting the vulture.[1] Volley still the vales
With hoarse artillery bellowing horrid sound.[2]
Muse![3] do we honour to the Brave who tamed
Uruguay's[4] rugged brood, and in its blood
Washed out the affronting of his King's decrees.
Aye me! Thou lust of Empire, such thy cost![5]
10   And you,[6] for whom the Maranhão suspends
Offerings of bursten jails and burthening chains,
Hero of heroes' brother![7] If in grief
Your fair America still yearns for you,
Favour my lay. So might it gain the power
To teach and train for flight these new-grown wings
Wherewith some day to raise you. In such sort
Fearful his natal nide afirst forsakes
Yon eaglet, humble earth anon to spurn
And seek a nearer view in empty air
20   Of the vast Blue the lightening-range beyond.
        Now from her bandaged eyen had rent the veil
Madrid long cozened:[8] on the new-found world
Severe reporter of the royal will
Catáneo landed; and to great Andrade[9]
Announced his succour ready for the war
And soon his host shall tread the tented field.
Ne'er could our General o'er a desert wold
Pursue his onward march till 'forced his power
With transport long long sought and sought in vain.
30   Erst had he o'er drear way of weary length
Sent his commands o'er every farthest part

To bring 'munitions for the war sore wanted.
   But while with thoughts opprest by long delay
Brooded his anxious brain a thousand cares,
Sad tumult breeding in his soul of souls,
Appears, led unexpected by his guards,
An Indian Brave in courier-garb bedight;
Who with strange ceremony humbly hands
The sealèd papers first all lightly-prest
With reverend gestures to his lips and brow.   40
   Well knows the faithful hand and feels content
Our noble chief who views, the paper torn,
Printed on wax that blusht with vermeil hue
High-born Almeida's[10] crest, the royal bird.
His missive warneth of his near approach
With transport needful for the march and fight,
Fire-breathing steeds and tardy steers to bear

The burthening yoke and drag the lumbering
    wain.[11]
No more delay! Right soon response he gives   50
To the returning courier of Castile[12]
And for him fixes trysting place and time[13]
When all the succours in his camp should meet.
   In fine they came, and Corps in sight of Corps
Our Chief defiled his troops along the plain,
That might the Spaniard view the large expanse
Swarming with noble hosts and sounding
    deadly arms.
Swift pass the squadrons and the guest meanwhile
Takes note of all and every sight observes
Propt on his staff.   60

              With light and agile tread
First past the soldiers of the avant-guard.
They lead the host to battle and their care
To scour the prairie and to assure the path.
Follow this host the men that must describe
The Camp and give it order, shape and size,
Remove it swiftly and as swift rebuild
The moveable houses with their lightsome roofs
And all the wandering City's square and streets.
Tugged by strong stallions straining at their toil
70 Work-heated, loud sonorous axles groan
'Neath heavy loads of dread artillery.
Then came forthwith begirt by all its guards
That fount of crimes, the treasury of the host,
Wherefore his crooked plow enfurrowèd leaves
The hind, who nought of Fame or glory knows,
And for vile lucre bartering blood and life
Moves, scantly recking why he moves, the war.
    Intrepid and in ranks immoveable
With lengthened pace, brows raised and eyen
        to front,
80 March with their mitred heads the Grenadiers.
They lead supported on the slender wheel
A new contrivance of the moulded brass[14]
Which, by deft fingers fed, with fast discharge
Multiplies deaths upon the slaughter-field.
    "Who may be this?" Catáneo curious speer'd,
"Adorned with snowy plumes in white and blue
Garbèd and deckt with manifold galloons
Whose breadth of bosom bears the precious
        Cross?"

To him Gerardo, who the Captain knew:
" 'Tis high Meneses,[15] more than every one   90
Strong armed in conflict, and in council sage.
All yonder infantry his warrior corps,
Flower of generous youth and noble blood,
Like him in azure white and gold is clad."

Pursued the Spaniard: "Prithee say who be
This vigorous ancient full of force and fire
In white and yellow 'quipt and brave with gold
Who heads and leads his Cannoneers afield?"

"Great Alpoim[16] thou seest. He the first
Amongst us taught the knowledge by what path   100
Heavenwards arise the curved and heavy bombs
Pregnant with fire and with what force adown
Crushing the City's roofs they fall and pour
From their rent flanks Death wrapt in fumy gloom."

Together followed in their father's track
Worthy such worthy sire, two noble sons.
Just Heavens! Illustrious Vasco,[17] must it be
That haughty billows must for thee prepare
Afar from me sad Death and watery grave?[18]
Ye Ocean-nymphs who saw if e'er ye saw[19]   110
His fading features and his frigid arms,
Ah! veil his eyes with verdant tendril'd hair.
Sad object of my fond and yearning woe,
As in my heart so live thou in my lay.

Thee and thy Grenadiers in scarlet clad
Nor less the Camp upon that day beheld,
Glorious Mascarenhas![20] Thou who still
In soft sweet peace that suiteth years less firm,
Impartial serving King and Fatherland,

120 Dictatest laws assuring general rest,
    The Toga's honour and the Senate's pride.
        Nor thou all-valiant Castro[21] didst prefer
    Ease in they patrial home: the Camp and arms
    Within that inclyt bosom fired anew
    The lofty valour of thy hero-sires.
        The last debouching on the martial field
    Were stout Dragoons with fear-despising hearts
    Prompt for the double trick and work of war
    Or 'mid the mountain-scrub afoot to fight
130 If so the ground require, and when required
    They veil in dusty cloud the general plain,
    Urging their fiery-hearted steeds to speed.
        The muster ended, straight our Chief invites,
    Pleased with the pomp and pride of mimic war,
    The Spaniards and his Captains, whom receives
    Within the purple tent, a mighty round
    Of splendid table hospitably spread.
    Banisht are carking cares while freely flow
    The wines of Europe in the golden bowls.
140 To the harmonious notes of ivory lyre
    Fired with the fury of the Muse divine
    Matúsio[22] of his hero-Captain lauds
    The high emprizes aye to memory dear:
    And future honours promising he sings
    Of blazoned scutcheons; on the potent shield
    E'en now he figureth, and his words portray
    Pearls and the titled honours of Grandee.
        Removed the festive tables various themes
    The hero-congress in discourse engaged.
150 There did Catáneo of our General pray

To tell from first beginnings what the cause
Of fatal tumults and the fresh campaign.
Still are the Fathers girt by rebel routs?
Who be their ruling head in peace and war?
For of their empire dark and deeply planned
Still Europe spake with accents vain and vague.[23]
Each warman in his place immoveable hangs
Upon the leader's lips in waiting ring
And silent all when thus begins Andrade.
    "Our latest Liege and eke the Lord of Spain   160
Resolved a single blow should cut for aye—,
As well ye ken, in this far coigne of land
Disorders bred by men of neighbour realms;
And by more certain signs divide us twain.[24]
They traced the limits where the Ocean laves
The barren littoral and Castilhos-chain[25]
Unto the nearest range, so mote the shed
Of water mark the boundaries of the rule.
Yours is the Colony;[26] unto us remain
The seven Reductions, wherein barbarous dwell   170
Peoples that hold yon vasty Orient Plain[27]
Which fattening Uruguay departs and bathes.
Who could have thought the few rude Indian men,
Sans discipline,[28] sans valour and sans arms,
Would block the path whereso our soldiers trod
And dare dispute the lordship of the land?[29]
    "In fine I gave not orders for a war
And our march frustrate they at length retired.[30]
Then with your General I determinèd
Enjoint to take the field when might appear   180
The sweet revival of soft vernal flowers.

Nor this the 'boldened Indians would endure
Who gathering fell upon a fort of ours
And them the Fathers[31] urge and company
For at their own discretion these alone
Can move or hinder battle fray and war.
The Captive Indians of our soldiers' arms[32]
In this my 'campment still you may behold.
    "Quitting our quarters we at length advanced[33]
190 O'er different ways by single aim impelled
To strike the centre of the rebel hordes.
By many a league of pathway asperous sore,
Thro' mires and woodlands, over hills and dales,
We reached a hindrance where fast stayed our steps
The rapid current of a giant stream.[34]
Here, on the opposing margent, rise to view,
In hosts innumerous, wild and barbarous tribes
Who from afar insult us and await.
I build me caracks and the curvèd rafts[35]
200 And make a feint my passage here to force,
While there my soldiers hidden ford the flood.
    "Already ended our emprize when lo!
Sent by your General's care, a courier came,
Bringing the news his battle had retired.[36]
Those Indian Braves had shown their warlike arts,[37]
Had wasted all the plain with Prairie-fires;
Me, too, he counsels to retreat awhile,
Till Time and Circumstance point other way.
To him in wrath — why hide it? — I reply
210 'Never the rearward step 'twas mine to tread.
Come at his pleasure, firm I meet my foe.'
    "Yet the fierce current and the form of ground[38]
Waged with us warfare never seen nor tried.[39]

All furious springing from its bed in broads
Lake-like it spread and with immoderate weight
Of water flooded, drowned the vasty plain.
My tents in sylvan trunks at first I picht,[40]
Then on the lofty branches: step by step
High in the windy realm we clomb to seek
Houses and homes amid the buoyant birds.   220
The densely-tangled forest now entwines
Verdant irregular streets and tortuous ways,
With squares disposed on one and other side
Cruised by canoes.[41] In such wise could we view
Where light commingled with the sombre shade
As through a glass transported and transposed[42]
From Adria's[43] waves the towering palace-piles
And gardens in a stranger element grown;
While lashed with oars and speckled by the sail
Sea-born Venetia's thoroughfares arose.   230
    "The silvery moon already twice had spanned,
Bending her burnisht horns the Heavens serene;
And yet the deluge-flood did not abate.
Within the watery waste all want was ours.
The Spaniard's succour threatened to be slow:[44]
Water and weather joined to cast us out:
Perforce I yielded and my host led home."[45]
    Unvanquishèd Andrade stayed his speech
And ere the meeting went its various ways
With royal orders hitherto right hid,   240
Surprising all, he fills their souls with joy,
The posts as suited best on all bestowing.
He to Almedia trusts the stout Dragoons
And "Campo das Mercês"[46] he names the site.

CANTO II

ARGUMENT

The march to meet the enemy—The prisoners are set free—
Two Indian parliamentaries Cacambo and Sepé attempt to
negotiate and fail—*Homeric*[1] *speeches:* Preparations for battle
—*Episode of Baldeta*—Victory won by the hero of the Poem.

Canto II

After the weary march of many days,
Reaching in fine a river flowing down
Slow and serene a fresh and winding vale,
The scouts that scoured the Prairie happed to find
A breathless steed whose breast and quivering flanks
Were bathed in sweat and fleckt with snowy foam.
    "We have our foeman nigh!" So spake his men
The experienced General: "Well I know how used
The voluble lazo which those Indians bear
10 Wherewith they 'tangle on the spacious plain
What horses they may need and when tired out
By the continuous gallop here and there
To the next comer fain they leave their own
Till rest and fodder pristine force restore."
    No error his: on the third day² appeared
The foeman formèd on his vantage-ground
Of chosen eminent hill: this swelling side
Was veiled with boscage and whose farther flank
Stood scarped and imminent hanging o'er a stream.
20   Noted our leader what strong site was theirs.
Meanwhile Meneses, who the nearest stood,
Thus spake him: "On these wastes 'tis ours to meet
More than we hopèd and to me it seems
By dint of battle only we shall force
Yon folk to yield them subject to our sway."
    Replied the General: "Try we first the might
Of love and gentle speech: an prove they null
Despite my wishes I must work my worst."
    Thus saying all the prisoner Braves in camp
30 Of every Indian tribe he bade his men
Deck with the garments of those brilliant dyes

The rude and simple savage loves so dear.
All he enfolded in a father's arms
And gave them freedom. With a general joy
They wind to seek their kith and kin and friends
While to his neighbour every brave declares
How large the heart, how liberal the hand
Of our unconquered Chief, our famed Andrade.
    And now dispatched by high command descend
Towards our Campment two of noblest strain,   40
Sans bows and quivers; but their heads and brows
Were crowned with tall and various tinted plumes
While kilts of feathers hung their loins around,[3]
Their ancles, arms and necks. Entered the tent
Without one courteous sign by word or deed
Sepé[4] the foremost. But Cacambo gave
After his fashion greeting new and strange
And straight began:[5]
                    "O Chief of fame well-known
Full sure thou kennest what a meiny drink
From haughty Uruguay's sinistral bank.   50
Albe our grandsires were, 'tis true, the prey[6]
Of fraudful Europe and from this spot we see
The greeny vales white glistening from afar
With our forefathers' unrevengèd bones,
I seek thee, left my weapons and my friends,[7]
So strong my trust in thee.[8] And long as might
Shall yield, great Sir!, to Right allow us see
If there be mercy for the blood, the life
Of these so many wretches. Long delay
Must lapse ere wait upon our wrongs Redress   60
While the large Ocean rolls atween our homes

Whereoer the groans and wails of woeful men
Lose all their breath of life. 'Tis in our power
Surrender to retard until what time
Shall royal justice to our homes restore
Sweet peace of olden days. And if Spain's Lord
Would grant large-handed to your King his land
Be the gift Corrientes,[9] Buenos-Aires
And others in these vasty climes he owes,
70   But he may never give him tribes of ours
And, grant such gift were his to give, I doubt
Thy Liege aught kenneth of the change he courts,[10]
I fear, indeed, he knows it not at all.
Whilome I saw the Lusian Colony
While in the tender tide of early years
When my old father with his tribal bows
The 'leaguering Army of Castilia's sons
Aided and measured with your men his might.[11]
And will ye, Portuguese, consent to yield
80   That domineering Fortress that commands
The watery Giant,[12] and with it resign
All claim to navigate its breadth of stream
Placed by the hand of Nature 'twould appear
To be your limit and your lasting bound?
Haply so; yet I doubt. Nay even more
These plains thou seest and this our patrial land
Without our toil of arms and sweat of face
What will they boot thy King? Here own we not[13]
Or deep-dug mines or yet the rushing flood
90   Whose sands are golden. All this wealth of ours[14]
That of our blessèd Fathers decks the fanes
Fruit of their industry and of the sale

Of hides and leaves; these riches all are theirs.[15]
With Empery o'er our bodies, o'er our souls
Heaven made their substance. Ours it only is[16]
To till and ear these old paternal fields[17]
With nought of payment[18] save the pauper store
In slenderest portions doled by sparing hands.
The humble hovel and the cotton cloth,
The bow, the grided shaft and gaudy plume   100
Compose our poor fantastic treasury.
Much toil and scanty comforts ours if any.[19]
Turn then, O Sir! return: nor farther go.
What wouldest thou more of us? Oblige us not
To fight upon this open field. It may
Cost thee a flood of blood one step to move.
Nor seek to see if these our shafts can pierce.
Thou seest the vain word 'King' affrights us not.[20]
Thine dwelleth far, afar; we Indian men
Own the good Fathers as our only Kings."   110
      He ceased to speak when thus vouchsafed reply
The illustrious General:[21] "Noble, generous soul,
Worthy to battle in a better cause,
Look! they deceive thee. Rase from Memory's page
These vain and fatal phantasies that feed
On ántique hatreds and ill-founded feuds.
Thro' me my Monarch speaks: hear, mark, attend!
For once the naked truth thy soul shall see.
Heaven made you free, but if your freedom mean
To live an errant and wide scattered horde,   120
Friendless, companionless and aye compelled
To wage a harmful war with armèd hands,
Right to confound with Might and in the wolds

To 'bide by venture, better far I deem
Thraldom than freedom offering bitter boons.
But neither slavery nor your misery wills
Our gracious Sovran who would see the fruit
Of his protection. And this absolute
Unbounded empire on you exercised
130   By vassal Fathers, like your vassal selves,
Know they usurp a harsh tyrannic rule.
Nor are they masters nor their serfs are ye.
The sovereign is your sire who wills you well,
Freemen are you as I; free shall ye live
In any region whither hence you wend.
But this fair country you to us must yield
For private welfare bows to public weal.
The peace of Europe claims the Sacrifice
And thus the King commands. Rebels are ye
140   Obeying him not; yet no rebellious souls,
Are yours full well I know. 'Tis the good Fathers
Who tell you one and all that you be free
And yet who use ye one and all as slaves.
They send your armies armed with orisons
To have the thunders of our fatal tubes
That level bulwarked walls; and are content
Afar to view the war while sacrificing
Your life-blood every chary of their own.
Before your faces I from them would tear
150   Their tyrant Empire o'er your climes, your homes
Where your simplicity hath throned them lords.
Dare they declare you have no King? Cacique![22]
What then the subject's oath of fealty?
Because he dwells afar you deem he cannot

Chastise you and deal chastisement to them?
Thou generous foeman! 'Tis one mighty fraud.
The Kings are throned in Europe. Yet take heed
These arms thou seest are but the arms of them.
Within a little while one sign from me
Can strew these woodlands and this broad
    wide plain   160
With palpitating semi-vital spoils
Of miserable men who never learnt
The causes dooming blood in streams to flow
And lave dure earth and lie in stagnant pools.
Call me not stony-hearted. While 'tis time
Reflect, resolve!"
              This said, our famed Andrade
Grasping the noble Emissary's hand
By manly mildness strove to melt his heart.
The thoughtful Indian musing long, at length
His arm and hand withdrawing spoke with sighs: 170
   "Ye, sons of Europe, would that ne'er the wind
And wave had borne you hither! Not in vain
Nature between ourselves and you hath spread
The water-wilderness, this vasty deep."[23]
   Haply had he pursued when stayed his words
Sepé, who breaking silence cried, "My brother
Hath overdone his duty. All men know
How Heaven bestowed these fair broad plains[24]
    we tread
Free to our fathers and in freedom we
From our forbears received as heritage   180
And free our children shall from us receive.[25]
We hate, we still refuse to bear the yokes,

Save that the Heavens vouchsafed to reverend
    hands.²⁶
The wingèd shaft shall judge between our feuds
Within a little while and shall your world
(If of humanity one trace remain)
Decide betwixt us twain if we defend
Thou justice, we our God and father-land."
    "In fine 'tis war ye want, war ye shall have,"
190 Rejoined our General. "You may now depart
For open lies the path."
                                    This said he bids
Cacambo take the guerdon of a sword
Garnisht with plaited silver and with gold
Wherein the work its worth of ore excelled;
A hat with ample flaps, a broad green belt
And last a costly cloak of verdant cloth
Flashing with yellow lace and crimson edge.
Then for Sepé he bade a bow be brought
Branteous²⁷ with ivory horns, and deckt and stored
200 With bright new arrows the famed quiver-case:
The self-same quiver he shall leave some day
When shrouded in his life-blood scant of breath,
Sans bow, sans charger shall the chief be dragged
Into our 'campment prisoner of war.²⁸
    The Indian brooded on past tales of wrong
And (flung the well-known quiver o'er his arm)
This wise replied: "O Chief! receive my thanks
For this thy gift of arrows; and I swear
Home and right speedily one by one to shoot
210 Mid smoky volumes on the battle plain.
By their sharp piercing thou shalt know thy bow

Or by their louder hurtling through the air."
    With such farewells the Braves went forth:
        our host
Disposed their ordered battle for the fray,
E'en as our General bade them. Either flank
Cover the serried squads of cavalry
While in the centre firm the footmen stand.
Like the fierce jaws the furious sleuth-hound shows
Garnisht with ivory files, smooth, sharp and white[29]
Our serried front the Indian foeman threats   220
With the keen-pointed bayonets begirt.
    Now blares the trump its blast of war. Now hear
Those silent deserts for the primal time
The Lusitanian drum; and now behold
Those tranquil airs a sight they never saw:
Our royal banners floating free of fold.
Springs from the frequent pits that fret the ground
Wherein the foeman crouched his lurking form
A cloud of Indians; gazed the eye in doubt
If the barbarians were by earth unwombed.   230
Thus errant Cadmus in an elder day
Saw, as the legends say, from teeming earth
The cruellest harvest grow beneath his glance.[30]
A loud and horrent shout of war they raise[31]
And towards our soldiers each his form inclines
While thousand thousand times the bended bow
Raineth from loosened string its shafty steel.
    A handsome stripling in his ignorance brave,
Whom public flattery's voice deceives and blinds,
Vain of his figure pricks him o'er the plain   240
To show with silly vaunt his plumes of war.

The shallow youngster of a strain obscure
Notheless had won the holy Fathers' heart.
They say, I ken not certain, him conceived
A barren mother by the prayer of Balda.[32]
And him for memory men "Baldeta" named.[33]
He prest a courser of a spotted hide
Fairer than forceful, whereon Nature's hand
A pleasant garden over all its form
250 Had traced and hence the steed was called
        "Jardim."[34]
The Father, saddened when the parting came,[35]
Gave it in sign of love; now on its back[36]
Wheeling at large with shafts uncertain shot,
He wounded many and he worried all.
    But if eternal infamy covered him,
Noble Gerardo,[37] all the fame was thine.
The boastful Indian whirls his steed when flies
Gerardo, meeting him in mid-career:
He fires his pistol and at once he makes
260 His blade reflect the splendours of the sun.
The youth affrighted reins his horse and halts
As one who hears the thunder, sees the bolt.
Trembling he wheels his steed towards his friends,
Hanging on either flank as if to fall;
While o'er the prairie here and there he leaves
His scattered arrows; floating by his flank
His plumery trails and by his flying hand
Loosened, the bridle coils upon the ground.
    Gerardo presses and his steel is near
270 When the Tatu-Guaçu,[38] most valiant sprite
Of all the fighting Indians of his day,

As to his bosom armed with squamous spoils
Of hideous Cayman[39] which his hand had slain,
Dashes between them.
                    Hard our Champion strives
With second pistol to lay clear the way
But vain the striving for the green-black skin
That decks and arms the stalwart Indian's breast
Is framed by Nature's art unpierceable.
His hand the shoulder smites and from the head
The coronal feathers strews upon the plain.   280
These bravest of the brave a band of ours
Separates; charging, trampling under foot
The routed Indians and in shortest time[40]
Cumbers the battle-field with hurt and slain;
And Victory decks our host with choicest bays.
    In flight precipitate casts away his arms
The enemy loath to face our volleyed fire.
Naught save his native speed may now avail him,
As Earth evanishes beneath his tread:
He flies and terror wings his flying feet   290
Calling on heaven and commending life
To priestly orisons. In similar way
Haply in other climes when roll adown
Their pale eternal snows the olden Alps
The headlong avalanche sweeps and overwhelms
Cattle and cottage. Desperate in his woe
The hurrying cotter climbs the highest tree
And sees the snows engulph his team and plow.
    A savage few, most famed in battle field,
The sole defenders of the fugitive horde,   300
Sustained the heavy weight of battle-brunt

Maugre ill-fortune. On one flank appears
Tatu-Guaçu who, fiercer in defeat,
And bathed in gushing blood pretends to turn
With single arm the fortunes of the fight.
Elsewhere Caitutu, haught and stark and strong
With manly bosom stems the foeman-flood
And like tall bulwarks shelters feebler friends.
　　　Nor less Sepé showed prowess on that day
310 Well known to all; in imminent deadly risk
He showed his naked breast and face unguarded
Enforcing bravery by his words and deeds.
Now all his quiver he had cleared of shafts[41]
And dexterous in his aim and fury nerved,
As many arrows as his hand let fly
So many blushèd red with Lusian blood.
Now with a sheaf of shafts anew supplied
He hies once more to fight anew the fight.
When the far-famèd Spanish chief who rules
320 Montevideo,[42] prompt with airy grace,
Inclines the bridle of his fleet-foot steed,
Spurs o'er the heapèd slain and wounded braves
Struggling with death and fronts his Indian foe.
Sepé who saw his charging poised his spear
And backwards bending arm and breast at once
Hurls it.
　　　　　　Between the body and the arm
Of the deft Spaniard speeds the quivery steel
And dents with harmless wound the hardened
　　　ground
While the light lame-shaft trembles long i' the air.[43]
330 But in the head and bosom of Sepé

Descends the Governor's sword severing the reins
Of his fierce courser. Startled flies the steed
And bears against his will, with fury wood[44]
His helpless rider o'er the battle-plain.
And or because the gory ground betrayed
Its tread or haply false the forehand fell,
The horse rolled over, hurling in its lapse
Sepé far headlong.
                         "Yield or die the death!"
Exclaims the Governor; but the proud Tapé[45]
Bends his bow spurning parley and his shaft   340
Speeds forth preparing for the enemy's death.
   This time 'twas his to miss. Wide flies the bolt
And with light feather fans the foeman's face.
The Spanish Chieftain may no longer leave
Victory doubtful; fires his ready hand
Point-blank his pistol at the warman's breast.
Scant was the space between; the bullet dealt
To the nude frame a dreadful mortal wound.
Between the shattered ribs exposed appear
The palpitating vitals. Thrice he strove   350
To raise himself from Earth and thrice he fell.[46]
His eyen already swam in Death's cold stream
And veiled them Sombre shade and iron sleep.[47]
Now, slain the great Sepé, no more resist
The timid squadrons. Fear no longer owns
Laws or command. Vainly in battle-front
Fain would the fleet Cacambo stay the flight.
Caitutu sorely hurt was forced to flee
The fatal field while from his severed veins
Tatu-Guaçu where'er he paces sheds   360

A stream of gore. The rest, the bravest lie
Wounded or downright slain.[48] Nor less descends
The victor's weapon on the Vanquished foe.
To the superior force of numbers yields
Cacambo saving all who mote be saved.

CANTO III

ARGUMENT

The Hero advances — Cacambo's dream which induces him to fire the hostile Camp — Episode of Lindóia's — Death of Cacambo — Lindóia's lament — The witch Tanajura shows by her magic the Lisbon earthquake, the rebuilding of the City by Pombal; the attempt to assassinate the King Dom José and the expulsion of the Jesuits.

Canto III

Already ours of Earth the ultime part
Had rolled[1] a brow that blusht incarnadine
To front the central light;[2] whenas the plain
Sown with the scattered seed of tomb-less dead
Beheld the errant City's sudden fall
As the drums sounded. Troubled sore and sad
Marchèd our General while his pitying breast
And generous soul could hardly bear to view
Those heaps of stiffen'd and exsanguine slain,
10   Butcher'd ambitious lawless rule to build.
    They gainèd distance and they open laid
Hostile and faithless lands until one day
Halting they pitched their camp in regions where
Valleys uncultivate for many a mile
To sight a weariness and sterile stretched
On either margent of a deepy stream.
Veilèd this vastest stretch of steppe and plain
A tangled growth of cane that clad the marsh

---

20   For fire's devouring maw a ready meal.[3]
    The Redskin habitant ever and anon
With his strange culture to the flames commits
Whole leagues of prairie and the burning lasts
As long as lasts the breeze which spreads the blaze.
Then on the herbage fire-renewed is fed
The herd immense descending from the hills;
And thus, by conflagration ay-renewed,
Art favours Nature and man learns the mode
To keep his flock in fat, the land in green.
30   But now, admonished by his espionage
Of our advancing march he keeps adust

The parcht burnt prairie in its horrid drought
Nor will he suffer for war's bitter work
The genial kindly fire and cooling ashes
To spread new gladness o'er the torrid soil.
    The steed till now with strength and spirit filled[4]
And food more generous never taught to need,
In all these climates save the greeny turf
Of the pure swart savannahs, languishes.
No more, caresst by rider's hand he curves   40
His forehand pawing earth, nor makes the vale
Sound with his neighing nor beflogs the air.
    'Twas midnight when the Heavens with heavy
      brow
Wrapt in a pauper cloak of gloom refused
Light to the world while murmuring was heard
Afar the river to the windy sough.
The realms of Nature lay respiring rest.
But lone and sleepless on the farther shore
Troubled Cacambo vainly woos repose.
In his perturbed and interrupted sleep —   50
Haply 'twas freak of Fancy — aye he viewed
The mournful image of the stript Sepé
Whose face was ghastly with the glaze of Death
Bathed in the flood of darkling gore that gusht
From the torn bosom while his livid arms,
Hoof-bruised,[5] betrayed his miserable fall.
His head all unadorned and at his feet
The broken quiver and the trampled plumes.
How changed, Alas!, from him, the brave Sepé
Who by encircling hosts of foes begirt   60
With streaming pores and deckt in dust and blood

Dealt dread and death!
                Sad words were heard to say:
"Fly, fly, Cacambo! What? Thou darest repose
While thus the foeman nears thee? Ah return,
Return thee to thy woods and in the caves
Paternal hide thy weakness and our shame.
Or if within thy bosom burn, perchance,
Desire of glory, in this hour of need
Bravely resist. Ah! thou who canst be brave.
70   Yes, thou who canst. Oppose thy hand the breast
Of Europe's fortunes: 'tis the very time
While torpid slumbereth all the hostile troop.
Spread fire and fumes around and let them pay
My blood and thy blood."
                    When these words were said
He disappeared amid the misty depths
O'er the tents waving high his smoky torch
And with his fiery finger showed the way.[6]
   Wakes from his swoon the Indian brave and springs
Out of the bending hammock sans delay.
80   His bow and arrows snatching up he smites
With foot the ground, to swim the mighty flood
He hies with breast to breast and dareth death.
Still float before his eyen the murdered form
Of his loved friend whose words still haunt his ear.
To a green trunk he hangs his varied plumes,
His bow, his clanging quiver and his shafts.
And where the current quietest rolls its course
Spreading in reaches o'er the ruddy sands,
In turbid thought, he dives and with the wave

Breast-high already, hands and eyes he lifts   90
To Heaven by him unseen, and to the waves
Commits his body. Saw the new emprize
Far in his silty grot the patrial Stream[7]
And with propitious gesture tilts his urn
To will its liquid crystal kindly smooth.
    The Fortune-favoured Indian unperceived
Upclimbs the farther stream-bank. Here he shuns
The guarded margent and with softest step
Hies in deep silence through the darkest shades
Seeking the part whence nightly breezes blew.   100
There, as his country's fashion is, he rubs
Two sticks together till he wakes the spark
And the brand casting on the crackling straw
Spreads fire amain.
               Now to the winds entrusts
His task Cacambo, flying opportune
The fire-light perils.
               But far o'er the bank
That hems the river when the flamy tongue
Begins to illume the shadows of the night,
Tho' by the watch and ward descried he feels
No fear and with his reckless daring trusts   110
By power of sturdy arm his life to save.
From the tall headland in the inky waves
Diving another time with downward plunge,
He sinks to seek the sands that floor the stream.
    In vain men shout, vainly they haste, they crowd
The margins of the water. He meanwhile
His feet outflinging and his nervous arms,
Pants through the foamy rings; and, once, but once

Poised on his hands he faces towards the camp
120   And in the tremulous mirror imaged views
The frenzied flames and joys the warren's joy.
      Not otherwise Ulysses, crafty foe,
Vain of the ruin which his guile had wrought,
Saw Troy's tall bulwarks reddening in the flame
And the perjurious city, smoke-empalled
Lean earthward bending slow and foot by foot
Down on its ashes topple.
                              Meanwhile spreads
The fire all fierceness, and the furious gale
Hurries with heaping hands the living lowe
130   Athwart the prairie here and there to spread.
Flies in a moment o'er the vasty flat
The fire up-blazing and in shortest space
Circles the startled 'campment of our host.
      The Chief armed cap-à-pie as he was found
From his tent sallying out with ready care
Hinders the progress of the hungry fire.
Of tents abandoning a few he bids
A breadth of ground be clearèd sans delay
Twixt fire and 'campment. Some now haste to cut
140   The inflammable culm, while others hurrying fetch
In ready pitchers-full the neighbouring wave.
      The bold barbarian tarries now no more.
He flies the foremost; winged by hot desire
To tell the tidings in great Balda's ear,
That self-same night he steppeth out his beat
And such his hurry when the fourth day broke,
Threading concealèd paths, he saw afar
His dearly lovèd land and well-known lea

Crowned by the spire whose vane the skies invades.
    But ah! he knew not what had Fortune's will   150
Reserved for his return, what wretched end!
How happier had he been! How better blest
Had he but spent the remnant of his days
In the free field and in the foeman's front
Or in the cinders of the burning tents,
Fired by his valorous hand!
                          Cacambo's bride
Of princely lineage was Lindóia[8] hight,
Gentle of bearing and from tenderest years
With modesty endowed. By softest bonds
Love hardly made them one, when sudden brayed[9]   160

The trump; and rudely tore their lively tie
Glory, that arch-deceiver. Or 'twas Balda,
That plotting brain, who sought himself to rid
Of the brave warrior's presence which he felt
Noyous and riskful; and aye since that Dawn
Bathed with its sympathising tears the pain
Of wedded lovers he refused consent
The spouse once more return to joy the arms
Of beautiful Lindóia; every time   170
The priest devised some pretext of delay.
In unexpected victory to return,
Such now his sole offence. The cautious Balda
Consent refuses that Lindóia hold
Free converse with her husband and decrees
A sombre cell should bar and ban the brave
Fro the Sun's veinèd light.
                         His parent princes,

His pitiful kinsman and the fast flowing tears
Of his despairing bride all failed to melt
180   The judge's stony heart. In fine by force
Of woeful yearning and of wistful love
And by the traitorous potion's hidden power,[10]
Given by the pity of the holy man,[11]
High-souled Cacambo died.
                             Of generous strain
In peace and dreadful war he, only he
Virtue's and Valour's bright example proved.
Bewept in secret, lacking honour due
Of princely funeral, in a spot unknown
A little dust his honoured bones conceals
190   If dust were granted on his bones to lie.
     Ye barbarous minions ah! at least conceal
The fatal tidings: ah! too soon shall hear
Lindóia filled with all the fears of love
The dread intelligence! And who now shall help
When life abhorring, forth she hies to find
The way that leadeth straightest to the tomb.
Nor wills she that her husband wait her long
In the dark Kingdom where Love may not love.
     But wrinkled Tanajura,[12] prudent grown
200   With years and many a trial, she whose breast
Maternal nutriment in happier days
To sad Lindóia's mother's mother gave;
She who the Future's darkling page could spell
In superstitious visionary eld,[13]
Who fro the ravisht sepulchre could pluck
The naked skull, the peeled and mouldering bones,
Within a grisly cave where ever flares

The green Candeïa-torch[14] led drowned in tears
Lindóia, nursling as a daughter loved;
And in a rusty cup[15] the pearly flood   210
From the live fountain drew. Thrice round the cave
Striding she circled; three times murmuring low[16]
Unholy verses with her hollowed jaws,
She breathed upon the water. Signed her finger
Silence, while in the bowl Lindóia gazed.

   As when the breeze that wisps the dark blue main
Droopeth awhile its light inconstant wings,
The waves fall slumbering and the plain reflects
In Nature's limning tall and beetling cliffs
And green-domed trees and cloud-rack high in air;   220
Not otherwise to scared Lindóia's eye
The watery borders of that bowl portrayed
The stream, the strand, the hills and dales that bore
A former Lisbon.[17] Lisbon still she saw
'Mid buildings shattered, crumbling to their fall,
Disordered Dame,[18] with torn dishevelled hair
Stumbling athwart the heaps of ruined homes.
Abandoned by her children, 'lone to mourn,
The Queen of Tagus solitary, sad
Among the yawning sepulchres would seek   230
Aid with her wistful eyes and still her eyes
Sightest[19] alone on this and other side
Walls overhanging and inclining towers.

   And more, she sees the Lusian Atlas[20] haste
Forceful to bear the hemispheral weight
On his red shoulders. From the skies serene
In silvery cloud a provident maiden form
Sudden descending with her bounteous hand

Presents the spirit of the constant strain,
240 Alcides' genius, who of monsters black
Riddeth the world and drieth his country's tears.[21]
The Giant grasps as trophies hairy spoils
Of hunger-maddened wolves besprent with gore
And crafty foxes. He commands:[22] forthwith
Obey the ready flames and where he bends
His benefactor steps, the waste of ruins
Incontinent opes a way.[23]
                              Lindóia saw
'Mid all the havock, as his finger becks
Upstart from earth[24] the high walls finishèd
250 And beauteous buildings. Fairer than before
Springs Lisbon from her ashes. Glorified
Be the great County[25] who with potent hand
Around her lofty brow had power to bind
The tremulous unsafe castles. Farther still
Prompt in the Tagus,[26] to bent irons chained
Striking man's vision with a terrible show,
And threating subject seas that powerful fleet,
That haught Armada.[27] Thro' the pitchy shrouds
White gleam the banners and loud groan the winds
260 Lashed to their poops, while floating fair and free
Hang from the cloud-rack and the billows kiss
The warlike pennons. From the horizon-line
On Ocean's breadth of azure breast appears
The painted *Serpent*,[28] masterpiece and gift
Of the new Western world; she wings her way
To seek the company of her buoyant friends
And from her offing now she hails aloud
Sintra's lost shades and highlands yet unseen.

Impatient of delay which may be death
The hirèd vessels moored along the shore   270
Receive within their flanks to distant climes,
Far from our Lisbon's pure delicious air,
Deported[29] Ignorance, Envy lean of limb
And garbed with trailing robes of sable hue
Discord and Fury. Old and vile as old
Hypocrisy, with her stealthy gait and show
Behind them stalking, doubts the while she walks
How human daring e'en such deed had dared.
The people point the finger, meanwhile she
With eyes bent earthwards fro the light of day   280
Hies fearful striving still her face to hide
With the torn corners of her cloaking rags.[30]
      Go! Daughter of Ambition whereso waves
And winds may drift thee: may thy hateful brood
Wander the waste of waters o'er. To thee
May lovely Europe port and roof refuse.
Right glad would I the Sun's fair light resign
Could but these eyes see Adria's[31] lovely land
Mindful of deepest injuries from her breast,
Outcast thee and from out their breasts outcast thee   290
Iberia, Gallia[32] and the lovely land
Apennine parts and gird the seas and Alps.[33]
      Seemed to Lindóia that the going forth
Of the vile monster left serener air
And purer breathing. Now the City shows
Distincter outline and renewèd form:
But on the farther side she saw — sad sight!
The taintless loyalty of Portugal
Walk with her robes of purity besmirched

300   By crimson traitorous stain. Beyond there rose
      With bandaged eyes, fro human sight concealing
      A blood-bathed poniard in her garment-folds,
      Bigotry, driving with relentless hand
      To noose and stake an age-bent hoary man.[34]
      Loud groans offended Nature and groans loud
      The credulous City, now ah-me! too late.
      The Church[35] in anger earthward drops her brow,
      Spurns, and blames, and heaps a dire revenge
      On the fell treason and the felon hand.[36]
310   Bound by the magic likeness, potent spell
      Enjoys the vain and fleeting forms nor dares
      Lindóia question aught. She sees destroyed
      The vile republic[37] and right well avenged
      Cacambo's murder.[38] Motionless, attent,
      She fed her hungry glances and desires
      Nor all she understood; when, lo! the crone
      Smote with her palms and made the waters quake.
      Now disappear in air the fancied towers
      And green-robed Earth: no trace of them remains
320   To show where such things were. In vain she seeks
      The ships; no ships are seen nor seas nor hills
      Nor e'en the place that bore the hills and sea.
          Lindóia yearning to recall the sight
      Renews her grief with groans and flowing tears
      Till silent Night-tide, with her pitying ear
      Hearing the mournful wails of hopeless woe,
      Rained down, departing, from her sable plume
      A gentle slumber, fresh with frigid dew
      And steeped her cares in sweet oblivion's spell.

CANTO IV

ARGUMENT

The Hero extinguishes the Prairie-fire, saves his camp and continues his march—End of the Lindóia episode—*Our* troops reach the city which is abandoned and burnt down by the Indians *at the order of the holy men.*

Canto IV

Saved from the midnight Prairie-fire his force,
The great Andrade drew him near the towns
When had he put to flight the Indian Braves,
Who strove each vantage ground of hill to hold;
Oft breaking, scattering by the headlong charge
The Tape chivalry whose dexterous hands[1]
Hurl with each spear a cause of double death
While their large whirlings gird the battle-plain.
    Deny they now as treacherous Calumny[2]
10 That to the barbarous Gentile host they taught
Our drill and discipline: deny they now
That traitor hands to savage distant tribes
By rugged paths thro' desert lands they brought
The sulphur dust, the hissing ball, the tube
Of bronze that roared its thunders from their walls.
Thou far-famed Blasco,[3] who didst see and tread
That region's utmost bounds, thou only couldst,
With the same hand that ruled the dread attack
And for each victory cleared and smoothed the way,
20 Paint for thy Liege's eyes the arms, the Siege,
The hate and fury of the incredible war.
    Upon the tall-topped crags at last they stood
Of the Bald Mountain, whose tremendous weight
Oppresseth Hades and whose giant head
Is hid in giddy height, no gales perturb.[4]
E'en as the voyager slow leaving land
Beholds the horizon's curving rim grow round
Till naught but Ocean with the sky confines
Nor aught appears save firmament and sea:
30 So he who looketh from those scarpèd peaks
Views only heaven while all the rest is hid

By swaths of frigid vapour dank and dense.
But when the Sun, beyond the eternal, fixt,
And purple back of flashing golden throne,
With hand creative makes to melt and rise
The ashy veil of floating waving cloud,
What scene of gladness for the glance! They[5] sight
From that high eyrie for a mighty span
Stretcht plains and prairie-lands with net-work cut
By shivering rivulets and by glassy founts   40
And lakes of crystal where aye loves to lave
His nimble pinions the soft playful wind.
The graceful swelling hill, the deepy dale,
The domed tree-islets weaving with their boughs,
A verdant theatre where man fain admires
Superfluous Nature's wealth of boons and charms.
Here patient Earth by husbandry reclaimed
Bares her rent bosom and the various plants,
Hand clasping neighbour-hand, enweave prolonged
Alleys and vistas where the lingering glance   50
Strays till the way is lost. The slow-paced kine
Tread loitering o'er the sward-plain and appear
(Amid the greeny hanging shades afar)
White-glancing houses and their lofty fanes.
    Meanwhile the Redskin lieges were convened
In the near village where the Saintly priest[6]
Would fain bestow Lindóia for a bride
On his Baldeta and for him secure
Murdered Cacambo's post and princely sway.
    Wide gape the gilded gateways that conduct   60
To the great Temple: in the neighbouring square
On either side in avenues are ranged

Arrayed in varied hues the sightly troops.
  With forehead villainous low and
      orange-stained,[7]
Cobé the misformed Indian leads the line,
Wielding with easy grip a weighty club
Wherewith in battle-brunt he fells the foe
As mighty tempests lay the laughing corn.
He leads the savage denizens of the hills
70 Who their own dead devour and ne'er consent
That frigid earth should dare fro them conceal
In her insatiate maw the stiffened corpse
Of the livid father or lamented friend.
  The second warman who in muster past
Was young Pindó,[8] who of the slain Sepé
The place had ta'en and still in brother-grief
For one so dearly loved yet unavenged
A black panache upon his head he bears.
All the other plumage is of vermeil hue,
80 The hue Sepé had aye in war preferred.
Him followed his Tapés, who most disdain
To die of years, the soldier's deepest shame.[9]
  Caitutu cometh next, of princely blood
Lindóia's brother. Not for strength of frame
Are famous those he leads, but such their craft
Of bowmanship, their arrows pierce afar
The bended beaks of painted parroquets
Winging the air:[10] nor 'scapes the certain doom
The fish with silvery mail that swims the depths
90 Of mountain torrents.
                    After him defile
The merry Guaranis of graceful mien:

This was Cacambo's ancient troop that wore
For dress the feathers of the firmament's hue
With cincture saffron-tinged.
                          And now Baldeta,
Puffed up with pride, leads forth his gorgeous troop
On Jardim's painted back; his lance mid-length
Is stained vermillion, whilst his head and limbs
Glitter in golden feathers to the Sun.
Cacambo's costly brand his flank adorns
And o'er his bosom gaily thrown athwart,   100
On the left shoulder bound, the baldrick green
Bears on his dexter flank the quiver's load.

    Pressing a courser black as sombrest night
Entered the latest in the principal square
Tatu-guaçu, ferocious Brave that guides
A jostling troop of savage chivalry
Who fight their battles all disorderly.[11]
They couch well-handled . . . ,[12] while the spoils
Of monsters mail their well-defended breasts.

    In his Baldeta did the holy Father   110
Review himself[13] and with low bows received
Outside the lofty gates the expected guest
Tedeu,[14] prompt and deft coadjutor,
With his companion of the tardy gait,
Brother Patusca,[15] bearing keys in belt,
By weight of vastest paunch to Earth attached.
Ne'er had the blustering sounds of cruel war
Torn him unwilling from his hours of ease:
Facile of morals and of softy heart,
By fellow feeling made to frailty kind   120
He bears resigned the joys of human life

Such as life grants us. Pleaseth him the world
Because it pleaseth, with effects contented
He knows not causes nor he cares to know.
Albeit in absence of some better man
His vulgar accents edify the herd,
And boorish cries and iteration vile
How of good father Adam the bad race
Decays by slow degrees, and gracious Earth
130   Grows worse with growing years.[16]
                                        Naught lackèd now
The couthless[17] revel ere its joys began
Save Triste[18] Lindóia. Long for her prepare,
Bedeckt in Innocency's snowy robes,
Festoons of flowers the fairest chosen maids.
Weary of waiting, from her lonely bower
The impatient many haste to bring the Bride.
Of crisp-haired Tanajura soon they learn
That drowned in tears the garden she had sought,[19]
Flying the presence of her fondest friends.
140   Caitutu feels a horrent shudder thrill
His veins and leaving in the square his troops
The well-loved sister through the treën shade
He seeks to see and yet he fears to meet.
    In fine they make the farthest innermost
Depth of that ancient forest sombre dark,
Where at the threshold of a caverned slab
Veils the hoarse waters of a welling stream
A bending bower of gelsomine and rose.
This spot most beautiful, most melancholy,
150   Had chosen weary of her wretched life
Hopeless Lindóia for her bed of death.
Reclined, as lulled in downy sleep, the Bride

Upon the verdant turf and varied flowers,
Hand-propped her cheek the while her arm was
    wound
Round the funereal Cypress glooming earth
With black lugubrious shades.
                         A nearer view
Shows that around her body is enrolled
A green-hued serpent that now glides now coils
O'er neck and arms and licks her lovely breasts.
Struck by the horrid spectacle they fly   160
And full of terror later stand afar[20]
Nor dare they rouse her with a cry; they fear
She start from sleep and rouse the deadly worm
To flight and flying hasten on her fate.
   But dexterous Caitutu trembling cold
To sight his sister's peril, sans delay
Bendeth his weapon's horns and thrice attempts
To loose the shaft, and hesitateth thrice[21]
'Twixt wrath and terror. But at length he twangs
The string and desperate speeds the grided bolt.   170
Lindóia's breast it grazes and it pins
The serpent's crest and deadly fangèd jaws
Fast to the cypress-trunk that near-hand grew.
Lashes Earth's surface with its flexible tail
The tortured monster and in tortuous guise
Curling the cypress round, black streams of gore
With livid venom streaked its jaws disgorge.
   The wretched brother raiseth in his arms
Ill-starred Lindóia whom he fain would rouse,
When by her death-pale cheek — ah! with what
    grief—   180
He spies the fatal poison-mark where struck

Upon her gentle breast the subtle fang.
Those eyes where Love had reignèd one short day[22]
Are glazed by death and dumb that tuneful tongue
Which to deaf winds and echoes many a time
Had told the long-drawn history of her wrongs.
    Caitutu yet forbids his eyes to weep
While bursts in deepest groans and sighs his grief
As o'er the entrance of the grot he reads
190 'Graved by a finger trembling to its doom
Another's crime that made her dight to die;
And everywhere resounded in its walls
The lost Cacambo's aye lamented name:
While still preserve her features wan and fixt
A something telling of a boundless woe,
A voiceless grief that melts the stoniest heart: —
So beautiful upon her face was Death.[23]
    Indifferent marvels at the bitter chance
By the strange rumour summoned to the spot
200 Stern-soulèd Balda, and his eyes review
The crowd of Indians reading thought by thought
How much can Terror! In one moment tears
Dry on each cheek and in more breasts than one
Die suffocated sorrows, moans and sighs.
And there it lay abandoned in the brake,
Left to the savage beasts and famisht birds
Nor dared a hand to grace the lovely form
With a few flowers, a pinch of pious mould.
    Thou haught Egyptian[24] who disdainedst swell
210 The lordly triumph of thy Latin foe,
If free thou fandest Hades' gloomy reign
Haply thy fancied vanity was fed

By hopes of barbarous pomp and queenly tomb!
But loved and lost Lindóia! Soon, I swear,
Shall thine injurious country wrapt in flames
Serve thee as funeral urn and furious winds
Mixed with its dust shall bear thy dust away!

    In dire confusion murmurèd the while
At such atrocious chance the pityful folk,
They say that Tanajura had described   220
Such death to her as sweetest way to die,
Haply had ministered the place and means.
Balda who waited long the time and mode
Of dreadful vengeance in his deepest breast,
Incites the people 'gainst the wretched crone
To pains exemplary: all joyous swarms
Round her the thoughtless petulant younger sort
Armed with the weapons their rough need supplies.

    But at this moment through the crowded streets
With sore affrighted mien an Indian runs   230
With hair fear-stiffened bursting from its knot,
Crying, "Fly, fly Oh friends this perilous land!
Already hard upon us stands the foe.
These eyes beheld them wind adown the hills
And come the prairie covering: and if now
I live the dreadful tidings to declare,
Due is my safety to my fleet-foot speed."

    "Vainly we hazard life in such a spot,"
Active Tedeu[25] cries, "A better plan
It were to troop within some other town: 240
Lose we the body so we save the head."

    "Thus be it then and thus the holy will
Of Heaven be done! And let him learn the while,

Yon contumacious enemy, how scant
Shall be his profit from the plundered flock!"[26]

Thus speaketh Balda and forthwith ordains
That all the squadded ranks at once retire
But first be fired the city and the fane.[27]
250 They go and going leave the hapless crone
Within a straw-thatched hut, while dire revenge
Prompts them with her the burning to begin.[28]
The shrilly shrieks of Tanajura's pangs
Rang echoing from afar. Towered and whirled
In the blue lift globed folds of lurid smoke
Ensanguining the golden light of day.
    With his huge chaplet loitering at the gate,
Devout and penitent stood before the throng
Brother Patusca who, when reached his ears
260 The first report, to save himself was first
And bid the dangerous land a long goodbye.
    However fast our General pushes on
Yet naught but cinders finds he still aglow
And red-hot rubbish where a city rose.
The flames devoured the wretched hovel-homes
Of the poor Redskins, and upon the ground
Smouldered and smoked each nobler edifice,
Delightful dwellings of the Reverend Men.[29]
    Entering the mighty Temple[30] on its floor
270 They find the holy images: the throne,
The golden throne where mortals' God Most High
(Long suffering, slow to slay the bad) adored,
Lay piecemeal on the ground. Turnèd his head
Our General troubled at the grievous sight.

His breast with anger filled, his eyes with tears.[31]
The troop of valiant men who girt their chief,
Dispersing here and there admired the size
Of the rich Temple; arches boldly spanned
Bases that firmly bore the lofty shafts
And forms and faces breathing from the stone   280
While on the vault the famed artificer
Had limned: — [32]

           But ah! what tempts me? this harsh
    strain
Despairs of such a brush to sing the charms.[33]
Genius of rude America that canst
Inspire the fury which transports my soul,
Now shall a stronger wing upbear thy bard.
My song shall pay with fame thy smiles of love.
List! while I promise that my lyre some day
Shall hang, thine altar's fittest ornament.[34]

CANTO V

ARGUMENT

Description of the frescoes on the ceiling of the Indian Church
—the Poet dwells upon the evils worked by "The Company of
Jesus"—The Hero pursues the enemy and surprises him in a
neighbouring town. Balda, *Tedeu and Patusca attempt flights*
—General submission of the *misguided* Indians.[1]

Canto V

Upon the vasty curvèd vault[2] had traced
The cunning artist's famed and dexterous hand,
Within a little space, cities and towns
And provinces and realms.
                                    From her tall throne
"Urbi et Orbi" law dispensing stood
The Company. Sceptres and Kingly Crowns,
Tiaras and the purple robes lay round
Sown over Earth. On one side heaped she had
Contaminating bribes: the further showed
10   Above the snowy altar hung on high
The grinded sword-blades dripping gouts of gore.
'Twas by her hand his towering walls amid
One of the Henry's loseth life and reign.[3]
'Twas by this hand, O Heavens! falls in vain begirt
By hosts of guarding men another Henry,[4]
His people's idol loved by all mankind.
Princes! his blood offends you one and all.
The dreadful monster planneth other crimes.[5]
Weapon your vengeful hands and let the share
20   With furbished point describe its furrowing lines
O'er her foul throne,[6] so man may never tell
To latest grandsons where her throne once towered.
         Far wandering earth and scattered everywhere
Her sons were pictured faring forth to lay
The strong foundations of expected rule
By twos and twos;[7] or on the tree-crowned hills
Of Tagus River or on strands remote
Where roam the Amazons with painted skins,
Strands, where the Monarch of the Waters foams
30   Spurning Earth's puny bounds and braves the Sea.[8]

Or sacred Ganges or the sombre range,
Virginal, ne'er profaned by foot of man,
Where Niless springs if any such springs there be.[9]
     With gesture innocent at the throne's foot
The free New World, America, was shown,
Who dragging fetters of enormous weight,
Sighs and her flowing eyes and bended brow
She may not raise for humbleness and fear.[10]
Before her lies her tribute, richest store
Of dazzling stone and silver ore and gold —   40
The fatal gold that buys her iron chains.
     Those distant azure seas and snowy sails[11]
With strange devices on the banners borne
Show how the Company claimeth kingly rights
When Commerce fares or Navigation flies.[12]
     Other times, other climates, other modes.[13]
Behold her far from home unlikest self
Enhabited in wavy length of skirt
Whereon barbaric work attracts the glance,
Breathing in China's air soft luxuries   50
Of Asian pomp and power while grave and slow[14]
She grants the Bonze to practice maugre Rome[15]
His worthless cult who gave the land a law.[16]
Japan admits her and behold she breeds
Dreadful domestic discord.[17] There she stalks
Amid the murdered and she points with pride
To sable robes whose edge is purple blood.
Thence from the wealthy ports in fine expelled,
Bending her glance upon the land she lost,[18]
In impious rashness she would trample down —[19]   60
Oh Heavens! What gloomy horrors: still remained

The picture all unfinished wrapt in shade.
Trembled the artist-hand to limn the scene
And on his paint-brush fainted every hue.

    Upon that other side where the haught shores
Bear wealthy London, see the fatal scene:
Dismayed the Thames[20] his blood-red stream
      devolves
Viewing the dark perfidious plot[21] that dares
Meditate heinous crime and wait and hope

70   Sky-wards to blow on shoulders flaming fire
And through the smoke-polluted clouds to scatter
The lordly Senate and the famous Hall.

    Amid the sable trunks of jungle growth,
By will and work of hers were seen dragged forth
To Afric's furthest wastes of burning sands
The Lusian valour and its high renown.
Oh fondly counselled as in valour fair,[22]
Thou generous youth by whom eternal grief
For weeping Lusitania was prepared.

80   Loved by thy lieges to uncertain climes
Thou farest to woo thy ruin, win a tomb.

    Now with the fell design full pleased she made
A Philip's hand her tool:[23] she drowned and
      whelmed
'Neath deep abysmal seas[24] and silenced well
Complaining tongues and patriots' holy lips
That dared the name of Fatherland pronounce.
And grew her might and firmer waxed her throne
By vengeance darkly dealt. To the broad main
Casts fro his hidden and polluted breast

90   Offended Tagus swimmers froze in death
While leaves his barque and hurries to the shore

The fisher struck with dread each time he drags
His nets long drawn by load of pallid corpse
Spoiled of sepulchral rites.
                        But while our troops
Upon the painted vault their vision fed,
A new emprize, a novel trick of war
The famed Andrade deep in thought devises.
   Hardly he waited till the dazzling sun
Upsprang and wholly left Earth's form opaque
When, forced his marches, to the other town   100
He fared the foe surprising. Now the Cross,
New Constellation ne'er by Europe seen,
Marked with its sloping limbs the passing hour.[25]
The brightly coloured morn serene and pure
Began embroidering on the horizont
The welkin peopled by the fleecy cloud,
When, opening wide the gates appeared the pair
Of Shepherd-Fathers[26] for the journey brisked,[27]

The wretched Indian flock abandoning   110
After exposèd to the rage of war.[28]
   The ravenous wolf that through the obscure of
      night
Slinks plotting treason to the timid sheep
When by pursuing bandogs brought to bay,
Burns not with choler and fell rage as burn
Priests Balda and Tedeu.[29] Gleeful throng
Around Patusca's stolid form the troops
As slowly moving on his tardy beast,
With provaunt laden followed he in rear.
Hung from his saddle-bow on either side   120
The savoury sausage, Europe's succulent ham

Rosy and white, while to his back was slung
That old and tried inseparable friend
Of every march — a mighty leathern flask.[30]
    Entering the Mission hastens to its fane
Invict Andrade, and with generous hand
The soldier-licence curbs while all protects he
With his great shadow, mild of heart and mien
In midst of victory.
                    Crowded round the chief
130 (Nor erred they) seeking safety and redress
The weeping mother with the guiltless sons,
And age-bent fathers and their timid maids.
Calmèd the tumult, straightway lay disclosed
Balda's vile treason and Tedeu's fraud,
The fell ill-famed Republic falls to earth.
Before the General's feet his couthless[31] arms
The rude American forthwith lays down
And recognizes law and humbles self
And prostrate hails the portrait of his King.

140 Uruguay![32] Men shall read thee. Veil some day
To come mine eyes black shades of night eterne.
Live thou and 'joy the light serene and pure.
Hie to the groves of Arcady nor fear
To step a stranger on an unknown shore.
There mid the sombre myrtles shedding shade
No funeral urn shall all Mireo[33] hold:
Raise from the foreign sky and o'er it spread
With pilgrim hand the wreath of barbarous flowers
And seek thy follower who shall guide thy steps
150 Unto that place which long thy coming waits.

TO THE AUTHOR[1]

Sonnet

It seems that I can see the massive flood
And the roving village floating in the water;
I loathe the crimes of the infernal scheme;
I cry for Cacambo and for the brave Sepé.

It is not a vain omen: people will read
About the war of Uruguay, as that of Troy;
And the tearful tale of Lindóia
Will sadden even the insensible heart.

Far away, Envy may infect a country rough and rude
With her wicked breath, but only her barely
Audible rumble will reach you.

Ah! allow my verse together with yours
As a weak vine that finds support on a trunk,
Also travel across the Universe.

By Joaquim Inácio de Seixas
Brandão, Doctor of Medicine
by the University of Montpellier

[1]Not in Burton; translated by editors.

Sonnet[1]

I enter Uruguay; I see the cultivation
Of the new lands by a clear genius;
But I reach the Majestic Temple, and I stop
Absorbed in the features of the painting.

I see the unfaithful Republic rise
On foundations of a niggardly authority;
I clearly see, if I look closer,
Usurper Cacus's dark cave.

Famous Alcides, it is up to your potent arm
To avenge the scepters and the altars:
Unsheathe your sword, strike with its blade.

And you, Termindo, carry through the winds
The great deed, because yours was
The glorious fortune of singing it.

By Dr. Inácio José de Alvarenga
Peixoto, a graduate of the School
of Law of the University of Coimbra[2]

[1]Not in Burton; translated by editors.

[2]The same who, years later, took part in the Inconfidência Mineira.

BIOGRAPHICAL NOTICE
of the Life and Writings
of José Basílio da Gama [Burton][1]

A notable want of trustworthy materials written or oral, especially as regards the inner life of man, is felt by the biographer of Brazilian worthies. I have remarked the same thing in the life of Camoens,[2] but he dates from three centuries whereas most of the illustrious colonials died within the last century. This remark will stand self-explained in the following Memoir.

José Basílio da Gama was the son of the Capitão-Mor[3] Manuel da Costa Vilas-Boas and of Dona Quitéria Inácia da Gama, both scions of noble families in the great and heroic Province Minas Gerais. He was born A.D. 1740[4] in the village of S. José do Rio das Mortes.[5]

The future poet's father died young leaving a family in straitened circumstances, and José Basílio was sent when thirteen years of age[6] to Rio de Janeiro. There Brigadier General José Fernandes Pinto Alpoim—celebrated afterwards in *The Uruguay*—[7] had offered to take charge of his education. The project was to make him a worthy son of Saint Ignatius and he presently began his novitiate for the cloister and canonical law.

The poet's theological career was suddenly arrested by the decrees of November 3 and January 19, 1759.[8] The great Carvalho, Marquês de Pombal, that minister "too great for so small a kingdom," forwarded to Brazil the Bull of Clement XIII and the Royal Ordinance expelling the Order of Jesus from the Portuguese dominions and confiscating their goods. The professed Jesuits were embarked and sent to Italy. The poet however had not taken orders and as a novice he was permitted to remain, but only on condition of breaking off all communications with the Company of Jesus.

103

Reduced it is believed to poverty, José Basílio now ardently pursued his studies of scholastic philosophy at the Episcopal Seminary of S. José. There his talents attracted to him the attention of men in power, especially of the Bishop D. Antônio do Desterro, for whom he ever cherished the liveliest gratitude, and the Captain General of Rio de Janeiro and Southern Brazil, Gomes Freire de Andrade, Count of Bobadela and afterward hero of *The Uruguay.* Unfortunately, this worthy man died broken hearted by the success of Spain and the loss of the Colony of Sacramento on January 1, 1763.[9]

This severe loss and the removal of two intimate friends from the coast to the interior determined José Basílio to seek means and the leave of his guardians in order to finish his studies at Coimbra. His stay there was short, he felt painfully his isolation in Portugal and the stigma of being a Jesuit and he resolved to visit Italy.

It is generally agreed that the disciples of Loyola, whose influence was still powerful at Rome, enabled José Basílio to visit the Eternal City, and there established him in a Professor's Chair at the Seminary. The *Biblioteca* [*Brasílica*][10] asserts that gratitude to the friends of his youth and a desire to see the world induced him to accompany them[11] to the Papal Capital. In 1763 he became a member of the "Arcadia" and took the poetical name of Termindo Sipílio.[12] This distinction he owed to some verses which he had composed in Memoriam of the Count of Bobadela, and to his powers as an improvisatory and a satirical writer. Yet he soon left Rome and impelled probably by *saudades,* nostalgia or [illegible word] found his way to Rio de Janeiro via Naples and Lisbon.

Arrived in the Brazil José Basílio was incontinently denounced as a Jesuit, arrested and was deported to Lisbon in a ship of war. There he was carried before the Tribunal known as "da Inconfidência," a Star Chamber and Court of High Treason, and he escaped only on condition of sailing within six months to Angola, in which pleasant Colony he was to reside until it should please Government to release him.

A profound horror of Angola seems innate in the Brazilian mind — I can hardly explain it, having found São Paulo de

Luanda a delightful residence after Fernando Po, where I was exiled without being a Jesuit or accused of High Treason.[13] Some attribute the poet's misfortune to the treachery of his old masters the Loyolites, who they say without explaining why, now hated him. But he was defended by the powerful Alvarenga family and he conceived in a happy hour the idea of writing an Epithalamium[14] to celebrate the nuptials of the Minister Pombal's daughter . . .[15] The harmonious octaves so full of pathos and spirit, celebrating the bride and her powerful father, who had restored its luster to the Crown of Portugal and had freed her from the deadly foes of her progress, were seen by Pombal. The Minister, a truer Maecenas than Richelieu, was pleased by them and saw the advantage of enlisting the ex-Jesuit or rather anti-Jesuit poet in his cause. He procured a remission of the decree of banishment, in 1771 he presented the author with papers of nobility (*cartas de nobreza e fidalguia*) and by an order dated June 25, 1774 he made his protégé one of his private Secretaries and attached him to the Ministry for Foreign Affairs.

With such patronage and with the full confidence of his protector, and with comfortable salary our author enjoyed some peaceful years during which he undertook and finished the productions by which he is best known. He brought out (1769) his favourite epic *The Uruguay*. He wrote a second smaller poem in 1791 called *Quitúbia* — its hero is an African brave who fought at Luanda with the Portuguese against their Hollander invaders.[16] He composed a "Cântico aos Campos Elíseos"[17] and addressed many *pièces de circonstance* to his great patron, and odes on family occasions. . . . He improvised a celebrated "Décima" full of wonderful conceits if not of poetry upon the subject of a medal which Pombal received in 1773 at his Quinta of Granja accompanied [sic] the Bull *Unigenitus* (July 21, 1773)[18] which extinguished the Jesuits. This medal had the arms of Clement XIV, of the Marquess of Pombal and the *Quinas*[19] of Portugal. An ode is also quoted describing the exploits of an Indo-American Chief — the Indian Tupac Amaru who bravely attempted to shake off the hateful Spanish yoke. . . . José Basílio is known to have composed several tragedies:

these with other productions never appeared. It is said that his confessor made away with them for which, says a Brazilian writer, the Reverend Man deserves to be roasted with his own sermons.

These productions obtained for their author a seat in the Academy of Portugal. But the friendship of his powerful patron caused his loss. On the accession of D. Maria I in 1777 reactionary policy set in, the Marquis of Pombal was deprived of his dignities and rusticated from Lisbon whilst his labouriously raised system fell to ruins. José Basílio behaved like a true man of honour. Instead of imitating other sycophants who basely turned upon the fallen minister he had the courage to address to him a noble Ode and to thank him for all his bounty and good.... The poet was compelled to throw up his employment with Government and [it] was again the spirit of Fortune who seemed to delight in driving him from place to place. As his youth was unhappy his age was miserable—sad penalty of telling truth. So untrue it is that "honesty is the best policy." Jesuitical influence began to receive strength and the "good fathers" attacked his Epic Poem the *Uruguay* in such odious pamphlets as *Resposta Apologética ao Poema Intitulado "O Uraguai."*... [20] They could not forgive their old pupil. Biographers also are unable to explain how it was that José Basílio, who showed himself so grateful to his patron Pombal, had attacked with such severity his ancient benefactors. The character of the poet leads them to suppose that he had found a something diabolical in the precepts and actions of the Jesuits, not to allow private considerations to influence his pen or past kindness to make him silent when a higher voice called upon him to speak. [21]

José Basílio, compelled to leave dangerous Lisbon once more, retired to Rio de Janeiro. There he found, happily for him, with the Viceroy Luís de Vasconcelos e Souza, D. José Joaquim Justiniano Mascarenhas Castelo Branco, at the head of affairs and a lover of poetry, in the Episcopal Chair of Rio de Janeiro. The Viceroy was also much attached to the poet Manuel Inácio da Silva Alvarenga, Professor of Rhetoric at Rio de

Janeiro, a native of Minas Gerais whose birthplace was two leagues from that of José Basílio. The two distinguished *mineiros* formed a warm friendship and under the powerful patronage civil and ecclesiastic they founded the Arcádia Ultramarina after the model of the Arcádia of Rome. Moreover in 1787 the favour of the Viceroy procured for him the honourable post of "Cavalier to the Queen."

This good fortune did not last long. In 1790 the literary Viceroy Luis de Vasconcelos was succeeded by the "sombre and anti-poetic" Count de Resende.[22] The new ruler was the antipodes of the old, a jealous and suspicious man, hating all liberal ideas and seeing in literary and scientific associations foci of disorder, which it was his duty by prison and banishment to put down. In 1791 the effects of the French Revolution extended to Minas Gerais and unhappily the great leader of the good cause was also a distinguished poet, Tomás Antônio Gonzaga, better known by his literary name Dirceu.[23] The Viceroy at once dissolved the Arcádia Ultramarina and threatened the discontented with loss of liberty.

José Basílio was again torn from his native soil and he returned to Lisbon. He led a simple and retired life, but the vicissitudes of Fortune had injured his health. He took to little purpose in 1792 the warm baths of Mó near Coimbra, and he [died in] Lisbon on July 31, 1795 at the unripe age of (60 says writer of life) 55. He became Corresponding Member of the Academy of Sciences, Lisbon, on February 12, 1795 and his name after that year does not appear upon the lists. He lived at Belém near the Secretariat which was then in Pátio das Vacas and his bones lie dispersed amongst those in the neighbouring parish church.[24]

NOTICE OF
THE URUGUAY
[BURTON]

The work by which José Basílio da Gama will live is his *Uruguay*. The subject of the poem is the Campaign which the Viceroy and General Gomes Freire de Andrade, afterward Count of Bobadela, conducted in 1756 against the Indians of Paraguay who were led... by the Jesuits.[1] On January 16, 1750 the crowns of Spain and Portugal had signed in the best of faith the "Treaty of Limits," a convention granting the Nova Colônia de Sacramento to his Most Catholic Majesty [Ferdinand VI of Spain] and in lieu of it to His Most Faithful Majesty [João V of Portugal] the Seven Reductions or Missions on the left (eastern) banks of the River Uruguay. The 30,000 Guarani or Tupi Indians were to be transported to the country south of the Ibicuí River. The catechumens refused to be bound by these stipulations. They fought with extraordinary energy and their plans betrayed the inspiration or great powers of imitation of civilized men. Of course the Jesuits denied having opposed the Portuguese (whom they hated on account of the Paulista *Bandeiras*),[2] but it was known that the cession of their establishments had injured their interests and they often protested against the measure to the Royal Audiences of Charcas and Lima and to the Governor of Buenos Aires for transmission to the Spanish Government. But their influence was gone.

It is possible that in his choice of a subject José Basílio was swayed by his aversion to the disciples of Loyola and by his desire to please Pombal. It is not less true however that he has succeeded in finding a patriotic theme and has discovered in his native land the materials of a national Épopée. He sings it is true the gross triumphs of Portuguese and Spanish arms, but he

also artistically bases the principal interest upon the unhappy
Red Man by his sketches of customs and character, by touching
episodes and by noble descriptions. Evidently not against his
will he betrays sympathy for the "noble savage," the victim of
priestly seduction.[3] And by the novelty of time and place he
awoke an interest in Brazil and contributed to establish the
national character which lost no time in forming itself. This
proves the originality of his genius: he despised the pen worn
subjects of remote antiquity, the Trojan clique, the

Race d'Agamemnon qui ni finit jamais,[4]

the exhausted subjects of Portuguese discovery and the roman-
tic tales made their own by Ariosto and Tasso.

Pereira da Silva[5] says rightly of this Epic Poem that the
author has left us a modern work in which the national and
New World Spirit shines with the purest luster and in which the
Virgin Continent is painted with the most lyrical descriptions.
Almeida-Garrett declares of him that he was "more national
than any of his Brazilian contemporaries" and that "the Brazil-
ians especially owe to him the choicest crown of their poetry
which in him is truly national and legitimately American."
High praise from the likes of this refined and critical genius.[6]

And truly the style of José Basílio merits all commenda-
tion. His verse is at once original, harmonious and suggestive.
In this as in his other poems he shows himself master of a musi-
cal style. His poetry is simple, never filling with the diffuseness
of the ottava rima. He has boldly preferred blank hendecasyl-
lables (*versos livres ou soltos*) when the national taste yearned
for Camoens's stanzas and for Alexandrines. The trial was
severe, but we must pronounce it a complete success.

In the cast of the poem the poet has unwound the origi-
nality of his genius. The beaten path of the dominant school
had laid down the rule of 10-12 or 24 cantos with the inevitable
accompaniment of mythology and allegory. He has preferred
the order of nature, and the freshness of the prairie and the
forest. By describing events which unfolded themselves under

his eyes, a sun familiar to him from his infancy and scenes amidst whose beauties he was reared he secured for himself, as Longfellow has to a certain extent in *Hiawatha,* that nameless charm of portraiture which men of the pencil call drawing from life.[7] His mode of connecting the episodes seems to have been borrowed from the Spanish "Romanceros" but the liveliness of his genius made the loan his own.

The Brazilian and the Anglo-American date from about the same age and it is amusing to compare the early poetry of the Latin with that of the Saxon. The colonies had got over the days when Thomas Welde of Roxbury and Richard Mather of Dorchester[8] thus recorded the Songs of Sion—

The rivers on of Babilon
There when we did sit downe,
Yea, even then we mourned when
We remembered Sion.

And when Michael Wigglesworth[9] could thus describe the "Day of Doom"—

They rush from beds with giddy heads,
And to their windows run.

But even in the 18th century the "Conquest of Canaan" by Timothy Dwight[10] and the stilted rugged "Columbiad" of the estimable Joel Barlow[11] prove how far superior in a similar state of civilization was the Muse of Brazil to her of the Anglo-Saxon settlements. That wrote poetry, this the *poem* of *prose.*[12]

"Tu Marcellus eris" is perhaps the prize of the *Aeneid,* and Ignez de Castro is the chef d'oeuvre of Camoens.[13] Here José Basílio gives us the beautiful description, and not an episode of the tragical fate of the two lovers Cacambo and Lindóia. All this part of the poem is notably treated. Nothing can be better than the scene where Cacambo—terrible name however!—roused by the Manes of his slaughtered friend Sepé rises at midnight, swims the broad stream and sets fire to the rushes with the object of crushing the enemy's camp. The audacious project fails; the brave flies to his native place where cast into prison and separated from his betrothed by the barbarous Balda, Chief of the Missions, he dies broken-hearted. The Jesuit would fain marry the hapless Lindóia to a wretched fellow, a putative son, when she in despair at her loss and taught by the Indian Sybil poisons herself Cleopatra-like by irritating a snake. The passage where she is found in sleep like death by her brother Caitutu is of all beauty, a poetic gem told in words that are [illegible word] nectar.

Critics are not favorably inclined to the fifth and last Canto and Wolf[14] thinks that the author would have done better to have exposed the political organization of the Hispanias and to have delivered his judgment upon the subject. But the description of the tableaux found in the principal establishment of the Jesuits leads to the artful enumeration of their deeds or rather their *crimes*[15] and thus it is essentially useful to the end inculcated by the poem.

The Uruguay ends with these noble, simple and prophetic words:

Uruguay! Men shall read thee, o'er my bones
Though some day brood th'eternal night obscure,
Live thou and 'joy the light serene and clear.
Go to th'Arcadian groves nor fear to be
A strange arrival on an unknown shore.
There mid the dark green myrtles freshly reared
Not all Mireu the sad urn shall hold.
Raise from the stranger sky, and on it shed
With pilgrim hand the wreath of barbarous flowers
And the successor seek to guide thy steps
Unto that place which long thy coming waits.[16]

In conclusion the only editions of *The Uruguay* with which I am acquainted are the "Épicos brasileiros publicados pelo Sr. Varnhagen," Lisboa, 1845;[17] this is illustrated with notes cultural and historical. The most recent is that published in Rio de Janeiro by Paula Brito, 1856.[18]

The translations are to come. Brazilian literature is a field which still awaits the foreign labourer. The name of Alencar[19] for instance is hardly to be found even in the text books and the anthologies—yet not the less it deserves to be known throughout Europe.

Santos, April 23, 1867 . . .[20]

NOTES TO
BURTON'S PREFACE

All notes are by the editors unless stated otherwise.

1. Francisco Adolfo de Varnhagen, Visconde de Porto Seguro, historian and literary critic; editor of *Épicos Brasileiros* (Lisbon: Imprensa Nacional, 1845), which has one of the texts of *O Uraguai* known to Burton, and from which the translator drew his belief regarding the proper order of the prefatory material (pp. 394-395).
2. Burton did not follow this plan. After the text of the poem are a "Biographical Notice" and "Notice or Appreciation."
3. "The latest description of this little port which has caused so much bloodshed and where even in 1874 a rebel government held its Head-quarters is in Captain Burton's *Letters from the Battlefields of Paraguay* (pp. 13-45). The Tupi-Guarani race has also been described by him in the notes to *Hans Stade* (Hakluyt Society, 1874)." [Burton]
4. "Some translate the word 'Uruguay' which the poet writes 'Uraguay' by 'Great River,' others make it 'Water of the Uru,' an aquatic bird in the Charrua tongue and others 'stream of the Cachuelas' or rapids." [Burton] In Portuguese, *cachoeira* means "rapids" or "waterfall" (see Burton's *Exploration of the Highlands of the Brazil* 2:37).
5. "*Histoire du Paraguay,* Paris, 1756; compare with Southey's *History of Brazil* (III, 39) and the Visconde de São Leopoldo's *Anais do Rio Grande do Sul.* (Chap. 3)." [Burton] This page of Southey does not refer to the matter in question.
6. "M. Remy (*The Hydraulics of Great Rivers,* London, 1874) increases the number to 'about 100,000.'" [Burton] It has been impossible to find additional information on this work.
7. "The modern Bobadela. Rare Ben Johnson was as unhappy in choosing 'Bobadil' as the divine William in his Falstaff (Fastolfe); both were names of good soldiers and gallant gentlemen. The viceroy's portrait placed by royal order in the Senate-house of Rio de Janeiro was deservedly inscribed: —

Arte regit populos, bello praecepta ministrat,
Mavortem cernis milite, pace Numam.

[Burton]

The Latin inscription can be confirmed in Varnhagen's *História Geral do Brasil antes de sua Separação e Independência de Portugal,* 7th ed. (São Paulo: Melhoramentos, 1962) 4:183n. The two lines can be rendered as: "He rules the populations with ability; in war he directs the operations; in battle you have the wisdom of Mars, and in peace of Numa."

8. Jean Antoine Victor Martin de Moussy, the "Dr. Martin de Moussy" mentioned by Burton in *Letters from the Battle-fields of Paraguay,* especially on pp. 32, 168. The work referred to above is *Mémoire historique sur la décadence et la ruine des missions des Jesuites dans le bassin de la Plata* (Paris: Douniol, 1864).

9. Francisco Solano López (1827-1870), dictator of Paraguay during the five-year war against the Triple Alliance (Argentina, Brazil, Uruguay). Burton traveled to the war zone as Her Majesty's vice-consul; this visit inspired his *Letters from the Battle-fields of Paraguay.*

10. Horace, *Ars Poetica (Epist.* 2.3), 133. Burton's quotation is truncated. He omitted the first word of the following verse, *interpres.* With the inclusion of this word, and, assimilating the context of the passage, the quotation is to be understood as meaning "you are free to enter the ground open to all if you do not dwell along the easy and open road, *and if you do not try to translate word for word as a slavish translator.*"

11. A pseudonym used elsewhere by Burton. See Introduction, "The Translator."

NOTES TO
THE URUGUAY

Notes not identified as Basílio da Gama's are by the editors.
Burton's notes have been lost. The places where he proposed to
add notes are indicated. In the majority, these passages had
been footnoted by Gama in the original.

CANTO I

1. Burton, note intended.
2. Burton, note intended.
3. The word *musa* ("muse") appears in all capital letters in the first
   printing, presumably for emphasis. This typographical arrange-
   ment is followed in most editions. A notable exception is the text
   that appears in Varnhagen's *Épicos Brasileiros,* an edition used
   by Burton, whose manuscript bears no indication for capitaliza-
   tion of this word.
4. Burton, note intended.
5. Burton, note intended.
6. Gama: "The Most Illustrious and Most Excellent Senhor Fran-
   cisco Xavier de Mendonça Furtado was Governor and Captain-
   General of the Captaincies of Grão-Pará and Maranhão, and he
   performed in the North of Brazil what the Count of Bobadela
   performed in the South; he encountered in the Jesuits the same
   resistance, and he overcame it in the same manner."
7. Mendonça Furtado, to whom the original edition of *O Uraguai*
   was dedicated, was the brother of Sebastião José de Carvalho e
   Melo, count of Oeiras, later marquis of Pombal, and of the in-
   quisitor Paulo de Carvalho. Gama: "In just one family the King
   has found three brothers worthy of sharing all of the load of gov-
   ernment. . . ." Burton, note intended.
8. Gama: "The Jesuits, on their own behalf and through their pro-
   tectors, had made a last effort to stop the implementation of the
   Treaty of Limits." For a response to Gama's charge, see Kaulen,
   Resposta Apologética, p. 22. For additional information on the
   matter, see Southey, *History of Brazil* 3:451, 472-475.

9. Gama: "His Excellency Gomes Freire de Andrade." This representative of the King was captain-general of Rio de Janeiro and royal commissioner for Portugal in the implementation of the Treaty of Limits. For his services, Gomes Freire de Andrade (1688-1763) was awarded the title of count of Bobadela. As to the Catáneo of the text, it is difficult to identify him. Varnhagen thinks the name of this minor character was Caetano. It is certain that he was a Spaniard. See I.51, where he is called a "courier of Castile." Burton, note intended.

10. Gama: "Colonel José Inácio de Almeida." Burton, note intended.

11. Burton has condensed vv. 47-48 of the original into one line.

12. Catáneo. See n. 9.

13. Gama: "The date was 16 January 1756, and the place was Santo Antônio-o-Velho." Burton, note intended.

14. Gama: "The Grenadiers were issued easy-to-load guns, which were the first to be used in Brazil." Burton, note intended.

15. Gama: "Colonel Francisco Antônio de Meneses, currently governor of the Colony." *Currently* refers to the time of the first edition, 1769. The colony was the Colônia do Sacramento, abandoned by the Portuguese, who returned it to the Spaniards in exchange for the Territory of the Missions. Burton, note intended.

16. Gama: "The Brigadier." Brig. Gen. José Fernandes Pinto Alpoim. It is said that as a friend of Basílio da Gama's family, Alpoim was in charge of the young man's education in Rio de Janeiro. Alpoim is also the author of textbooks on artillery. Burton, note intended.

17. Gama: "Vasco Fernandes Pinto Alpoim, son of the General and a special friend of the author, died as a lieutenant-colonel, while still quite young, aboard a lost ship, on a trip from the Colony to Rio de Janeiro."

18. Burton, note intended.

19. Burton, note intended.

20. Gama: "Fernando Mascarenhas, Captain of Grenadiers, afterwards Sergeant Major, currently serving in the Senate." Rodolfo Garcia, in his notes to the commemorative edition of *O Uraguai*, states that there was no officer by that name in Gomes Freire de Andrade's force: "The poet seems to be referring to João Mascarenhas de Castelo Branco, captain of the Regimento Velho of Rio de Janeiro . . ." (p. 124). Burton, note intended.

21. Gama: "Lieutenant-Colonel Gregório de Castro Morais, of a very illustrious family, was governor of Rio de Janeiro at the time of the invasion of the famous Du Guay Trouin." The latter was a Norman privateer who captured Rio de Janeiro in 1712. Burton, note intended.

22. Varnhagen, in *Épicos Brasileiros,* identifies this Matúsio as Sgt. Maj. José Antônio de Matos, secretary to the governor of Rio de Janeiro (p. 400). The original may have been intended as a play on words based on the Latin adjective *matus,* "drunk," a pun that would not be entirely out of place in the celebrations described in the text. For other instances of plays on words by Gama, see the notes to II.250 and III.157. Burton, note intended.

23. Gama: "The Jesuits have had the gall to deny throughout all Europe what has just occurred in America in our own time within the sight of two armies. The author experienced this in Rome, where many persons sought him out expressly to learn well-founded news of Uruguay; evidencing a strange contentment in finding an American who could inform them minutely of what had happened. The wonder, caused by the strangeness of facts so well known among us, brought forth the first ideas of this poem." The author of the *Resposta Apologética* reacted indignantly to this passage (p. 52). Burton, note intended.

24. Gama: "The Treaty of Limits was signed on 16 January 1750, between His Royal Highness D. João V of Portugal and D. Fernando VI of Spain. This treaty hurt the Society of Jesus in that it transferred to the Portuguese those lands that the Company had held as its property on the Eastern side of the Uruguay River." See *Resposta Apologética,* p. 52. Burton, note intended.

25. "The demarcation began at the mouth of a little stream which falls into the sea, and rises at the foot of Monte de Castilhos Grande; from thence it proceeded in a straight line to the mountains..." Southey, *History of Brazil* 3:443.

26. Colônia do Sacramento.

27. Burton, note intended.

28. Gama: "As it was thought at the time." Burton, note intended.

29. Gama: "When the officers in charge of the demarcation reached Santa Tecla, they found the Indians in arms, and these Indians impeded their progress." For a different account of the same episode, see *Resposta Apologética,* pp. 54-56.

30. Burton, note intended.

31. Burton, note intended.

32. Gama: "These prisoners totaled fifty; some of the more important ones were sent to Rio de Janeiro, where the author saw them and also spoke to them. They confessed quite innocently that the priests had escorted them to the Rio Pardo, and had stayed on the other side of the river. They were surprised because the Portuguese treated them so gently. They said that the Fathers kept warning them in their preachings that the Portuguese were possessed by the devil, and that all were sorcerers. In case they ever

killed a Portuguese, to make sure that he would not be alive again, it was necessary to bury the head at least one hand's span away from the body, a practice that they followed religiously."

For a response to this charge, see *Resposta Apologética,* p. 60. Gama would have been eleven years old when the Indian prisoners were sent to Rio (1752).

33. Gama: "The Portuguese General left Rio Grande de São Pedro on 28 July 1754."

34. Gama: "The Jacuí River. They reached it on September 7th." Burton, note intended.

35. Gama: "A type of boat, used by our men in that region to cross the largest and the deepest rivers. They are made of cowhides. The cargo goes in the bottom, with men on top of it, and the horses swimming beside the boat. The Indians, who are very robust and great swimmers, draw these boats by means of a rope, whose end they hold between their teeth. Whoever goes inside holds the other end of the rope, releasing it more or less, as needed." Burton, note intended.

36. Gama: "The Spanish troops withdrew because the cavalry was weak. They had gone a long way along the river, and the grass had been eaten by the Jesuits' cattle. Additionally, they had no desire to enter the Missions, nor were they entirely persuaded of the King's intentions. The most serious reason for the doubts was related to the letters that came from the Court of Madrid, amidst secret machinations; the Jesuits were involved in all these dealings and conspired more than ever." Burton, note intended.

37. Burton's alternate version of line 205 is prosaic: "The Indians' military discipline."

38. Gama: "All those woods and meadows, for many leagues, are swampy and subject to these floods. There are whole nations of Indians who build their huts and live in trees. They are quite deft at going up and down the trees without ropes or steps of any kind. The trees are very tall, and for the larger part of the year, their roots are under water."

39. Burton, note intended.

40. Gama: "Perhaps a similar deed cannot be found in History. All the Count of Bobadela's constancy was necessary to keep an army lodged for two months in the trees." In his edition of the poem, J. Artur Montenegro, not always reliable in his information, here comments sensibly: "The data collected by the author were no doubt exaggerated. Good sense rejects the possibility of the army climbing trees in the forest and leaving to the mercy of the flood its artillery, provisions and impediments, when it is certain that by marching a few leagues it could have reached the heights of

the valley and tranquilly waited there..." (*O Uraguai* [Pelotas: Echenique Irmàos, 1900], pp. 90-91). Burton, note intended.

41. Gama: "Small boats used by the Indians, made of one log; in them the Indians came secretly to barter with the Portuguese and the Spaniards." Burton, note intended.

42. Burton, note intended.

43. *Adria* = Venice. See III.288.

44. Gama: "*Post bellum auxilium*," or, "The reinforcements arrived after the war."

45. Burton, note intended.

46. *Campo das Mercês* can be translated, "Field of Rewards."

CANTO II

1. Words underlined in the Argument are not found in the text printed by Varnhagen and are the translator's contribution. See also Arguments of Cantos IV and V.

2. Gama: "On the tenth day of February 1756." This is the date of the Battle of Caaibaté, the central action of the poem. Burton, note intended.

3. Burton, note. In Burton's notes to Albert Tootal's translation of *The Captivity of Hans Stade of Hesse,* we find a detailed description of the feathers and other decorations worn by the Indians (pp. 139-140).

4. There existed several Indians named Sepé who fought in the war. According to Rodolfo Garcia, the one depicted in the poem is probably one José Tiarariú, who died in combat on 7 February 1756 ("Notas Complementares," pp. 132-133). See below, lines 309-355. As to Cacambo, there was a real Indian by that name, who was captured and died in prison. For a discussion of how Basílio da Gama created these two Indians, mixing fact and fancy, see Antônio Cândido, "A Dois Séculos d'*O Uraguai*," in *Vários Escritos,* pp. 161-188. Burton, two notes intended.

5. Gama: "All of the Fathers learned the Indian language and, against the desires of the King, forbade the Indians to use any other language besides their own. In this manner communication with the Portuguese and the Spaniards became impossible, and what happened in these backlands became unfathomable. And, what is worse, the Jesuits flaunted this kind of tyranny all over Europe:

> *Nescia gens nostri vivit ....*
> *.......... ad interiora venire*
> *Regna vetent homines cupidos audita videndi.*
>   Vanier, *Praed. rust.* Lib. XIV."

Gama has quoted from the French Jesuit Jacob Vanier, *Praedium Rusticum* (Paris: J. Le Clerc, 1709); the passage can be rendered as: "People do not know us; people curious to see what they have heard are forbidden to go to the interior of this country." The author of the *Resposta Apologética* uses the same facts with a different interpretation (p. 72). Burton, note intended.

6. Gama: "The Portuguese bring to our homes all the present disgraces. Remember that in times past they killed your forefathers. They killed thousands of them all over, without sparing even innocent children." This passage was supposedly quoted from instructions given to the Jesuits, who would preach such ideas to the Indians. The author of the *Resposta Apologética* has an emotional rebuttal: "Mr. Gama, here the prose and the verse do not agree. The Indian, who in the poem is introduced speaking, complains about the killings perpetrated by the Spaniards on their forefathers, and the note attributes such killings to the Portuguese. What nonsense! The same thing is imputed to one group when you write in verse, and to others when you write in prose" (p. 78). Burton, note intended.

7. Gama: "They had express instructions from the Fathers not to meet the Portuguese. The Jesuits characterized the Europeans as 'those who are against us; when they want to talk to us, we will avoid them, running away from Spaniards, and even more from the Portuguese.... If they ever want to talk to us, there must be five Spaniards, no more. There must not be Portuguese, for if there are Portuguese, their fate will not be good. The Father, who is one of the Indians, and knows the Indian language, will be the interpreter, and in these conditions all will be done, because this is the way God orders us, and if we do not obey, the devil will take charge.' *Instruções, etc.*" Gama's indicated source has not been identified. Burton, note intended.

8. Gama: "We do not go where you are, because we do not trust you." Burton, note intended.

9. Scanned "Co-rri-en-tes" by Burton, the area bounded north and west by the Paraná River and east by the Uruguay, capital of the province of the same name in modern Argentina.

10. An allusion to the exchange of the seven reductions for Colônia do Sacramento.

11. A reference to the siege of Colônia do Sacramento by the governor of Buenos Aires in 1735-1737.

12. Colônia do Sacramento on the river Plate.

13. Gama: "The Fathers made the Indians believe that the Portuguese were people without law, who adored gold." Burton, note intended.

14. Gama: "Those riches were immense: their houses and their temples were magnificent, in a way that cannot be imagined in Europe. We do not even have to go so far: in Rio de Janeiro the Fathers had, among others, the Santa Cruz farm, so large that none of the most wealthy families had funds to buy it. In this property they had more than one thousand slaves, and countless head of cattle. In spite of all this, it is a fact that no money was found when their properties were confiscated. A few days after their departure, a former lay brother, who was a bricklayer, reported to the Count of Bobadela, claiming that he was going to show him the place where he had, by order of the Fathers, hidden the money. In fact, all that was found was the place in the foundation of the new church. As soon as they saw the layman had left their company, they performed one of their tricks." Burton, note intended.

15. Gama: "The Indians and the Spaniards use *maté* as the Chinese use *tea*. This important trade was entirely in the hands of the Jesuits of Paraguay. They raised the trees that have those leaves, and shipped it in leather containers all over Spanish America. This trade alone brings yearly revenues of many millions. All this is accomplished with the toil of the poor Indians." The *Resposta Apologética* denies the charges (pp. 98-99).

     Gama quotes from Vanier (see n. 5):

     "Semina nos colimus faustis quae jacimus agris."

     Literally: "We tend the seeds which we plant in the fertile fields."

16. Burton, note intended.
17. Burton, note intended.
18. Gama's note is a brief, truncated quote from Vanier.
19. Gama: "It is not even necessary to go to Uruguay to have proof of the excessive toil of the Indians for the benefit of the Fathers. Between the village of Santos and the city of São Paulo there is a very steep large mountain range which cannot be climbed on horseback. The Count of Bobadela, the best rider of his time, fell twice right at the beginning of the climb, and he was using horses that were chosen from among many others. Everyone climbs on foot with the horse following. The Fathers, as they had made vows of poverty, were happy to go up and down lying in hammocks, carried by the poor Indians; and never would they pass there in any other fashion. In Europe this may sound fantastic, but the author certifies its veracity." The author of the *Resposta Apologética* has a strong answer to this "inept accusation" (p. 106). Burton, note intended.

20. Gama: "These expressions are not poetic embellishments; all that the author has the Indians say actually happened." Burton, note intended.

21. The speech by Gomes Freire de Andrade, which starts at this point, was criticized by the author of the *Resposta Apologética* on literary terms. Father Kaulen had this to say: "Speech by the general poorly conceived by the poet" (p. 111).

22. Burton, note intended.

23. Lines 171-174 are among Gama's most famous.

24. Quoting from a document not fully identified ("Carta Sediciosa"), Gama tells his reader: "God gave us this land, and to our forefathers, and therefore we alone own it for the love of God."

25. Burton, note intended. His alternate version of line 181 is somewhat obscure: "And free shall they unto our seed descend."

26. Gama: "This mixture of sacred and profane, or better said, the use of Religion for personal ends, has always been a Jesuit trait. Consider with care the following line:

> *Non gentem imperio, sed religione tenemus.*
> Vanier."

The quote states that "we do not hold these people in the name of the government, but of religion." Father Kaulen, in the *Resposta Apologética,* has a strong reaction to this note (p. 113). Burton, note intended.

27. *Branteous* (?). This word may derive from the obsolete, northern English dialectical form *brant* ("steep," "lofty"), perhaps in the sense of "erect," "straight." Another possible reading is *Acanteous,* a reduced form of *Acanthaceous,* from the Greek *Acantha* ("thorn"), with a meaning of "thorny, similar to the acanthus plant" (*Oxford English Dictionary*).

28. Burton misread lines 201-204, translating the past perfect form *deixara* ("had left") as future tense; this led to misapprehension of another past (*foi trazido,* "was brought") as a future. Sepé had been imprisoned while attacking the fort at Rio Pardo (see line 205, below). At the end of Canto II Sepé is killed, not imprisoned.

29. Burton's alternate version of line 219; his first rendering is "Garnisht with ivory files, smooth, piercing white."

30. In the extended simile, a reference to the Phoenician prince who was legendary founder of Thebes. According to tradition, Cadmus killed a dragon and sowed the monster's teeth, which turned into warriors.

31. Burton, note intended. It might be related to the custom of yelling in combat. See *The Captivity of Hans Stade,* p. 151n.

32. Gama: "Father Lourenço Balda was one of the most tenacious leaders, who most instigated the Indians to rebellion." Balda was born on 16 July 1704 in Pamplona, Spain, and joined the society of Jesus in 1726. The *Resposta Apologética* calls Gama's charge a calumny (p. 116). Burton, note intended.

33. Gama: "The Jesuits of America were not so scrupulous as those in Europe pretended to be. It was quite easy to spot the Indian girls who enjoyed special favors from the priests in each village. In the same manner, the young men of the family could be easily detected. In Asia it was the same. Read the letter from the Bishop of Nanking to Benedict XIV." The *Resposta Apologética* calls these charges "bigger calumnies" (pp. 19-24).

34. Burton, note intended. The reader could legitimately expect an explanation of the pun found in the original, where we see a horse's spotted body that looked like a garden as a reason for the name Jardim, especially because Burton did not translate the name of the animal.

35. Burton, note intended.

36. Gama:

> .... *quem candida Dido*
> *Esse sui dederat monumentum et pignus amoris.*
> Virgil, *Aenid* (V. 571-572)

The passage quoted by Gama appears in the description of war games in which young men take part. One of the lads has a spotted horse (similar to Jardim); another rides a horse "which fair Dido had given him as a gift (to remember her by) and as a token of her love." Burton, note intended.

37. The same character who appears in I.89.

38. Gama: "*Guaçu*, in the language of the Indians, means *big* ["great"]. Some prouder Indians add this word to their names, which sounds among them as among us, Charlemagne, Alexander the Great, etc." "Big Armadillo" is the translation of the brave's name, which appears elsewhere (II.303; II.360, IV.104). The Indian as well as the current Portuguese usages stress the last syllable of each word of this name. Burton does not always respect this pronunciation. The text marks his variations, stressing the accented syllables. Burton, note intended. See *The Captivity of Hans Stade,* p. 62.

39. Gama's note gives the zoological classification of the animal. Regarding *jacaré*, used in the original, see *The Captivity of Hans Strade,* p. 162; *The Exploration of the Highlands of the Brazil* 2:177-178. Additionally, see Burton's preface to the poem, p. 41. Burton, note intended.

40. Gama: "In spite of the fact that the Fathers had armed the Indians and done everything possible to discipline them, still they were unable to withstand regular troops. It would take much cruelty to send those poor wretches to their death only in the name of ambition and whim." The *Resposta Apologética* has a rebuttal (p. 125). Burton, note intended.

41. Burton's alternate version of line 313; his first rendering is "Now he had emptied all his quiver-store."

42. Don José Joaquín de Viana, governor of Montevideo. See I.24. For a less heroic version of this scene, see Southey, *History of Brazil* 3:479-480. See also Varnhagen, *Épicos Brasileiros*, pp. 30, 402.

43. Gama's line ("E treme fora muito tempo a hástea") is a literal rendering of one line of Alonso de Ercilla y Zúñiga's *La Araucana:* "Tiembla por largo espacio la hástea fuera" (X.26). See also note to IV.85.

44. *Wood* (archaic) = insane.

45. Here (and also in IV.6 and IV.81) the translator took metrical liberties with the name of the Indian nation, which is normally stressed on the first syllable. Burton, note intended.

46. Here, as in IV.168, Gama uses the contrast of a thrice-attempted action and repeated failure. There is a certain element of magic related to the number three. Contrast the two cases just discussed and III.211-212, where the magical meaning is more obvious.

47. Burton, note intended.

48. According to Gomes Freire de Andrade's *Diário da Expedição*, of the 1,700 Indians, 1,500 were killed and 154 were made prisoners; the Spaniards suffered 3 men killed and 10 wounded; the Portuguese, 1 killed and 30 wounded.

CANTO III

1. Gama: "This is said hypothetically." The poet apologizes for his flowery speech. Burton, note intended.

2. A simple prose rendering of the first two and a half lines would be: "Our remote part of the world had already turned its gory face to the center of light." Using the word order of Gama's verse —a rather unusual one in Portuguese—the translator almost lost control of his text.

3. Burton has condensed vv. 17-20 of the original into three lines, omitting v. 19: "E leves juncos do calor tostados..." (And light sedges parched by the heat).

4. Burton's alternate version of line 36; his first rendering is "The Courser filled thus far with strength and sprite (life)."

5. A word misunderstood by the translator, or an intentional play with the word *pisados* of the original? The past participle of *pisar* ("to step on something"; also, "to hurt," "to wound") refers to Sepé's arms. Burton rendered the words *pisados braços,* in the context of a cavalry charge, as "hoof-bruised arms." By combining the two meanings of the Portuguese word, the translator improved the original and may reveal a subtle understanding of the language.

6. Burton, note intended. The translator might have discussed how Indians produced fire, as he did in a note to *The Captivity of Hans Stade of Hesse* (p. 126). The translator has created a startling metaphor in this verse, which literally would read: "And with flames he points the way."

7. The river Uruguay.

8. For a discussion of spelling of Indian names, see the Introduction under the heading "The Present Edition." Lindóia's name does not seem to be a Tupi word, and it is reasonable to imagine it was created by the poet, using the Portuguese *linda* ("beautiful") with an ending that might make it sound like a Tupi name.

9. Burton has condensed vv. 160-161 of the original into a single line without significant loss of meaning.

10. Gama: "Only those who have never read History can ignore how often the Jesuits use this expedient in the most difficult cases. Nobody doubts that Innocent XIII's death, when he was ready to put a stop to irregularities committed by the Jesuits, was their work. Cardinal Archinto had the same fate. In Rome it is common knowledge that Cardinal Passionei died of a 'Jesuitic accident.' This incomparable prelate had said, on occasion, that he hoped to see, before his death, the total extinction of the Company. The Jesuits had the haughtiness to write this epitaph for him: '*Dominico S. R. Card. Passion. S. J. superstes.*'" Literally translated, the epitaph says: "To Cardinal Domenico Passionei, (dedicated by) the surviving Society of Jesus." For a very strong reaction, see the *Resposta Apologética,* pp. 133-138. Burton, note intended.

11. Ironic allusion to Balda. See II.243.

12. Burton, note intended.

13. Gama: "The Indians gave themselves entirely over to superstitions, and they held to be not only probable, but certain all the extravagances that can be imagined in this matter: they lived in the most crass ignorance. They were only allowed to learn what could be useful to the Company. The doctrine taught them could be reduced to a fear of Hell lest they disobey their *Holy Fathers.*" Burton, note intended.

14. The Portuguese text has the word *candeia* ("torch," "lamp," or "candle"). Burton, note intended.

15. Burton, note intended.

16. Contrast the magic connotation of an action performed three times here and its use in II. 350-351 and IV. 168.

17. Gama: "It is well-known how the Jesuits took advantage and attempted to profit from the public calamity [the Lisbon earthquake of 1755] to consternate and subdue the populace for their own pernicious interests. So if it had not been for the serene spirit of our Most Gracious Monarch, truly imperturbable, and the constancy of his most enlightened Ministry, Portugal would have remained forever buried in the ruins of Lisbon." The reference is to the government of the famous Sebastião José de Carvalho e Melo, count of Oeiras and marquis of Pombal, the prime minister of José I of Portugal from 1756 to 1777. His power was consolidated after the great catastrophe.

18. *Dame.* Refers to Lisbon, as does Queen of Tagus below.

19. *Sightest* (*sic*).

20. *Lusian Atlas.* Refers to Portugal.

21. *Alcides* = Hercules. An allusion to Pombal and the expulsion of the Jesuits. Burton, note intended.

22. Gama: "Steps taken after the quake." Burton, note intended.

23. Gama: "Clearing the city."

24. Gama: "Reconstruction of Lisbon, owed entirely to the greatness of His Majesty's heart, and the tireless spirit of His Excellency the Count of Oeiras." See note to III. 224.

25. Obsolete form of *count* (here, the count of Oeiras). Burton, note intended.

26. Gama: "The Royal Navy, with the great progress that we witness, is but one of the glories of this most fortunate crown, and this glory is due mostly to the zeal of His Excellency Francisco Xavier de Mendonça Furtado." The note clarifies the passage and gives the poet an opportunity to say something favorable about the prime minister's brother, to whom the poem is dedicated.

27. A literal rendering of this passage (254-258) in a less unusual word order: "Farther still, ready in the Tagus and chained to bent irons, the powerful and noble ships, threatening the sea, give the eye an impressive sight." Using a gerund (*striking*) in the main clause, Burton made the passage sound fragmentary. Burton has an intended note after "Armada" in line 258.

28. Gama: "Warship built in Rio de Janeiro during the government of His Excellency the Count of Cunha, with beautiful carvings made from assorted woods in several colors, an uncommon work and unique of its kind." This boat, officially called *São Sebastião* and

launched on 8 February 1767, became known as *Serpente* because of the large figure of a dragon on her prow. Gama dedicated a sonnet to her launching. See José Veríssimo, *Obras Poéticas de José Basílio da Gama* (Rio de Janeiro: Garnier, n.d.), p. 241. Burton, note intended.

29. Gama: "Only posterity will be able to evaluate this action, which will always be remembered as the most brilliant among all of our acclaimed Ministry. Without this measure the Kingdom would never have escaped from the ignorance in which they [Jesuits] held it." This clearly refers to the expulsion of the Jesuits from the Portuguese Empire in 1759. The *Resposta Apologética* debates the issue (p. 179).

30. Burton, note intended.

31. Gama: "Because of the famous interdict of Paul V the Jesuits, who under scabrous circumstances wanted to have the Curia on their side, left Venice, where they finally returned half a century later. It seems incredible that the Venetians have totally forgotten this action." In a dispute over the extent of papal jurisdiction in Venice, Pope Paul V had excommunicated the Venetians and sought to lay their dominions under an interdict (1606). See the *Resposta Apologética*, p. 180. For *Adria*, see I.227. Burton, note intended.

32. Gama: "When the author wrote these verses he could hardly imagine that most of what is described in them would be fulfilled during his own lifetime. We further have the good hope of seeing the rest fulfilled shortly." The Jesuits were expelled from France in 1764 and from Spain in 1767. The order was abolished in 1773 by Clement XIV. It was restored in 1801 by Pius VII. Burton, note intended.

33. Burton, note intended.

34. Gama: "Gabriel de Malagrida, diabolic martyr who was left behind by the Company as a last demonstration of its rebellious and fanatic spirit. The Jesuits circulated among their friends a picture with the words '*V. P. Gabr. Malagrida in Portugall. pro fide occisus.*'" The last part of the note tells us that "Father Malagrida [was] killed in Portugal in defense of faith." The information provided by the poet is inaccurate and biased. Gabriel Malagrida was not "left behind by the Company" when it was expelled from Portugal but rather held in prison by direct order of Pombal. He had been accused of several crimes, including a plot to kill the king. Malagrida's real "crimes" were mostly his opposition to Pombal's colonial policy and later the publication of a booklet that attributed the earthquake to divine punishment: *Juízo da Verdadeira Causa do Terremoto que Padeceu a Corte de Lisboa no 1º de Novembro de 1755* (Lisbon: Manuel Soares, 1756). The

prime minister accepted the book's thesis as a personal insult, and five years later, in 1761, Malagrida was dead. Burton, note intended.

35. Gama: "He was turned over to the secular court." The note still deals with Malagrida, and it intimates that the missionary was a common criminal. On Malagrida, see the *Resposta Apologética*, pp. 22 ff., 186-188.

36. Burton, note intended.

37. The "República Guaranítica."

38. Where Gama has *morte*, "death," Burton used *murder*, making the charge against Balda more obvious. Regarding this accusation, see the *Resposta Apologética*, p. 129.

CANTO IV

1. About the Tapes, see note to II.339. Burton, note intended.

2. Gama's note begins: "The Jesuits, who today roundly deny the truth of facts so evident, in other times made ostentation of the same." The poet then quotes several verses from Vanier's *Praedium Rusticum*. Burton describes the military regimentation of the Guaranis in his *Letters from the Battle-Fields of Paraguay*, pp. 32-33. Burton, note intended.

3. Gama: "The Marshall Michel Ângelo de Blasco, chief engineer of the Kingdom." The "engineer" was a Genoese employed by the Portuguese crown for the demarcation of limits in South America. Burton, note intended.

4. Burton, note intended.

5. *They* (*sic*). Burton could have been thinking of the Portuguese *olhos*, "eyes," which he translated as *glance*. It could also refer to the troops; line 22 tells us that *they stood* on a mountain.

6. Gama: "Balda." Burton, note intended.

7. In Gama, "Stained with *urucu*," the fruit of the annatto tree (*Bixa Orellana*), from whose pulp a dye is extracted. The Indians used it, as the text makes clear, to decorate their bodies.

8. According to Mário Camarinha da Silva, a name inspired by Santiago Pindo, one of the tribal chiefs who signed the truce at Jacuí on 14 November 1754. *O Uraguai* (Rio de Janeiro: AGIR, 1964), p. 77.

9. The passage can be translated literally as: "With them go his Tapes, who throw themselves into battle and despise dying of old age." Burton changed the second line subtly, perhaps projecting his own feelings as an old soldier. Regarding the Tapes, see notes to IV.6 and II.339.

10. Another passage inspired by Ercilla's *Araucana* (X.18, 7-8). See also note to II.239.

11. Burton, note intended.
12. A word is missing in Burton's translation; "lances," "missiles," or "javelins" are possible readings, which would render the Portuguese *lanças* and also fit the meter.
13. Playing on the etymology of *review* ("see again") and using the word with an obsolete meaning, Burton managed to echo the Portuguese "Revia-se em Baldeta o santo Padre."
14. The Jesuit Tadeu Hênis, author of a diary of the war, written in Latin. Basílio da Gama regularly misspelled the first name, making it "Tedeu," but he keeps its two-syllable character. Burton scans the word in three syllables. Burton, note intended.
15. Gama: "I have drawn this portrait from the live model—a lay brother of the Company—whom the author used to know." Rodolfo Garcia asks: "If the poet was never in Paraguay and Patusca never in Brazil, where did they meet?" *O Uraguai* (commemorative edition), p. 144. The historian fails to consider that Gama does not state where he met such a person; he further fails to see the literary character of the work, concentrating instead on the polemical aspects. The name Patusca is related to the adjective *patusco*, which means "fun-loving, funny, extravagant." We may notice that Gama used the normally feminine ending *-a*, referring to a man, a usage common in insulting nicknames. For a reaction to this caricature, see the *Resposta Apologética*, p. 193.
16. Burton, note intended.
17. *Couthless* probably means rough, unpolished. Also used by Burton in V.136 and in his *Personal Narrative of a Pilgrimage to Al-Medinah and Mecca* (New York: Dover, 1964), I.19.
18. *Save Triste* [Lindóia]. The adjective is not in the original, but the translator's contribution does not alter the spirit of the text.
19. Gama: "The Indians lived in utter misery, and hardly had the things absolutely necessary for life. The Fathers nevertheless lived in abundance, and had delightful gardens, where they withdrew their spirits tired of working in the vineyards of the Lord." The *Resposta Apologética* discusses this charge, p. 197. Burton, note intended.
20. Burton's line reads, "And full of terror later then stand afar," which is redundant and metrically incorrect.
21. See note to II.350-351.
22. *One short day*. The adjective was added by the translator.
23. A famous line, most likely taken from Petrarch's "Morte bella parea nel suo bel viso," *Trionfi* (Torino: Unione Torinense, n.d.), I.172. There is an exclamation point at the end of the line in the Portuguese original.
24. Gama: "Cleopatra." Burton, note intended.
25. *Tedeu*. See note to IV.113.

26. Burton omits the following line in the original, also spoken by Balda: "Falta-lhe a melhor parte ao seu triunfo" (The best part of his triumph is lacking).

27. Burton, note intended.

28. In lines 250-251, Burton changed the singular subject of the original (Balda) to plural.

29. Burton, note intended. This is a passage where anti-Jesuit comments would fit the text, and Burton would not have refrained from expanding on this matter.

30. Gama: "Our men still managed to save the Temple, of which the ground plan and design were sent to His Majesty. The Fathers had ordered the images smashed, and the Sanctuary was reduced to pieces." For a reaction, see the *Resposta Apologética,* pp. 203-206.

31. Gama: "The General found it hard to believe that the precious ornaments had been woven in that country, until he was shown one that was found near the Sacristy, which was unfinished in the loom." There was no reaction in the *Resposta Apologética.* Burton, note intended.

32. Burton, note intended.

33. Burton misunderstood this passage, rendering *intento* ("I try to do," "I attempt") as if it meant "to tempt." The two lines can be freely translated as "[the artist] had painted . . . but what am I trying to do? The hoarse voices / cannot follow the traces left by the brushes." Having begun an objective description, the poet stops suddenly, switching to the first person—a change even more clear in the subsequent lines. In this sudden change of focus, Gama was echoing Camoens in the *Lusiads,* in the description of Vasco da Gama's arrival in Lisbon which brings the narrative to an end. Similarly, Gama's narrative ends here, in spite of the presence of one additional canto. See *Os Lusíadas,* X. 144-145.

34. A similar invocation appears at the end of the last canto (V. 140-150).

CANTO V

1. Notice how the translator implicitly takes a stand against the Jesuits in the argument of this canto, describing the Indians as "misguided."

2. The poet goes back to the description interrupted in IV. 282. Gama: "The exploits of the Jesuits were not buried only in Uruguay. Any reader who may be puzzled by the paintings on the Temple's wall should think about the Church of their Roman College, and about the one in their House for Professed Jesuits; the fact that they are all masked under the guise of religion does

not prevent them from being more disdainful and insulting." The author of the *Resposta Apologética* calls these descriptions false (p. 213). Burton, note intended.

3. Gama: "Henry III, assassinated by Fra Jacques Clément. Is there anybody who is unaware of the part the Jesuits had in this? The trial of Father Guignard is well known, and how the Company has been defending this worthy member to this date. See the Company's Authors, and above all Jovency." Fr. Jacques Clément was a Dominican who murdered Henry III of France in 1589, perhaps as one of the many results of the king's alliance with his Huguenot cousin, Henry of Navarre (who later became Henry IV). As to Guignard, he was a politically active Jesuit; one of his students made an attempt on the life of Henry IV. "Jovency" refers to Joseph de Jouvancy, S.J. (1643-1719), a famous scholar whose editions of Latin and Greek classics were widely used; he coauthored *Historia Societatis Jesu* and wrote the *Christianis litterarum magistris de rationi discendi et docendi* (Paris: n.p., 1692), which became the official manual of classical studies in the society. Gama was clearly assembling a large number of facts, not all related, and making them appear as evidence of serious crimes. For a defense, see the *Resposta Apologética*, pp. 216 ff. Burton, note intended.

4. Gama: "In the death of Henry IV, the Jesuitic hand was able to hide itself better, but this was not the case in the two previous instances in which similar crimes were attempted. Father Varade, Superior of the Company in Paris, was responsible for poor Barrière going astray; he took him to his cell, gave him a blessing, confessed him, gave him communion, etc. The Jesuits of the College of Clermont, and in their Church of Saint Anthony, corrupted the spirit of Châtel by means of lectures, conferences, meditations and spiritual exercises." Gama's substantial note has practically nothing to do with the poem. Furthermore, he goes from one accusation to another, without any logical progression. All of the cases were probably well-known at the time. Châtel was the student of Guignard (see n. 3 above) who tried to kill Henry IV. Barrière was a soldier who also tried to kill the same monarch. Henry IV was finally murdered in 1610 by a man named Ravaillac, who had no connections with the Jesuits. In this canto more than in any other, we find the two parallel texts of *O Uraguai*, one in verse, one in prose; up to the fourth canto they run together; here they do not have the same close relationship. Burton, note intended.

5. Gama: "Just remember the afternoon of 5 January and the night of 3 September, so tragic for France and Portugal, that covered with mourning these two Kingdoms." In addition to the crimes

already mentioned, here Gama alludes especially to the attempted assassination of José I of Portugal on the night of 3 September 1758. Several members of the nobility and a few commoners were executed in early January of the following year. Pombal tried to implicate the Jesuits in this plot, without success. Father Gabriel Malagrida (see III. 304 and 309) was accused of being the main plotter, and three years later the prime minister managed to have him executed. For a discussion of the attempt on the life of José I, see Southey, *History of Brazil* 2:540-541. For a rebuttal, see *Resposta Apologética*, p. 230 ff. Burton, note intended.

6. Gama: "The Company's throne is in Rome. This is the center of its power. There its General receives news of what is occurring all over the world, and from there with the greatest despotism he sends his orders to the end of the world. To exterminate the Company from the Provinces is to attack the branches: it is necessary to cut off the roots. The treasures of the two Indies helped support the credit of the Jesuits in Rome. Fortunately the trend seems to be the total extinction of the Company." For a discussion of these charges, see the *Resposta Apologética*, pp. 237-239. Burton, note intended.

7. Gama: "In Portugal the Jesuits were called the Apostles, and they scrupulously respected the ritual of going in pairs." This is a strange note, when we consider the poem had anti-Jesuitic purposes. Father Kaulen, in the *Resposta Apologética*, deviated from his usually very serious tone to say: "This was a great hallucination, Mr. Gama!" See pp. 242 ff. Burton, note intended.

8. Gama: "The Amazon River flows into the sea with a mouth that is eighty leagues wide; it flows with such force, that it projects fresh water for many leagues into the ocean." The *Resposta Apologética* had no objections here. Burton, note intended.

9. Gama: "The Jesuits even boast in their histories of having discovered the origin of the Nile." Burton also marked this passage for a note. These lines of the poem must have been extremely poignant for Sir Richard, who also searched for the sources of the Nile, and failed. See Fawn Brodie, *The Devil Drives*, pp. 119-120. For Burton's treatment of the Nile in his translation of the *Lusiads* by Camoens, see Frederick C. H. Garcia, "Richard Francis Burton a Luís de Camões: O Tradutor e o Poeta," *Ocidente* (Lisbon), Nov. 1972, pp. 79-80. For a discussion of Gama's statements, see the *Resposta Apologética*, p. 245.

10. Gama: "Words cannot explain sufficiently the bondage in which these Indians lived. See the fragments of the Letters written by the Count of Bobadela, quoted in the *República*." Burton, note intended.

11. Gama: "The Jesuits in Brazil had a magnificent frigate, ostensibly used yearly by the Provincial to visit different parts of his Province; but the actual use of the frigate was for a very active business among the several cities (of the Province). . . . The author saw this frigate many times, and boarded it. It flew the colors of the Company, and also had excellent artillery. On entering and leaving port, it was granted all the honors reserved for the Crown warships." The *Resposta Apologética* has a discussion that starts with the following heading: "What is said about the Jesuit frigate in Brazil is refuted," p. 249.

12. Burton, note intended.

13. Gama: "The Jesuits of China in the year 1645 took advantage of the division of that great Empire between the two pretenders, in order to deliver it to the Khan of the Tartars. As a reward they were elevated to the rank of Mandarins, and bedecked in the rich garments and necklaces that can be seen in the prints left us by Father Bonani in the *Catálogo dos Religiosos,* etc."

The reference is to F. Filippe Bonani, *Catalogo degli ordini religiosi della chiesa militante. Espressi con imagini e espiegati con una breve narrazione* (Rome: Rossi, 1706-1707). The *Resposta Apologética* discusses this charge. Burton, note intended.

14. Burton, note intended.

15. Gama has three notes related to this line. The first: "Furthermore, they used the word *Tien* (Heaven) and *Xamti* (Supreme Ruler) in reference to the true God; and also had some rituals for the dead." The second note is a simple explanation of the meaning of the word *Bonzes* (plural in the original): "Priests of China." The third note: "And clearly in spite of Rome, which tired of fighting the animosity of the Jesuits for more than a century. . ." The note continues with details of the long controversy. All three notes are in one way or another related to the controversy of the Chinese rites (essentially similar to the discussions regarding the Malabar rites in India), a controversy that lasted for centuries. For the specific charges, the *Resposta Apologética* had strong answers (p. 261). Burton, one number, presumably intended for one note only.

16. Gama: "Confucius." He is the man "who gave the land a law." Burton, note intended.

17. Burton, note intended.

18. Gama's note cites the Jesuit Vanier, regarding the expulsion of the Jesuits from Japan. Kaulen, *Resposta Apologética,* reacts with indignation (p. 269). Burton, note intended.

19. Gama: "The Jesuits, with their mental reservations, did not doubt at first to trample the crucifix in order to retain that extremely lucrative trade. Anyone who may desire to be more informed on

this matter, read the travels of Mr. Duquesne, sent to the East Indies by Louis XIV, vol. 3, p. 81." The reference is probably to Abraham Duquesne, *Journal du voyage de Duquesne aux Indes Orientales, par un garde-marine servant sur son escadre* (Brussels: n.p., 1692). There were other printings before Gama's time, and an English translation (*A New Voyage to the East Indies, in ...1690 and 1691...*) was published in 1696. Burton, note intended.

20. The original has *Tâmega* instead of *Tâmisa* ("Thames"), perhaps an etymology created by the poet. Varnhagen corrects the original and points out the error, reminding the reader that the "Tâmega is a Portuguese river" (*Épicos Brasileiros*, pp. 64, 404). Burton has the right river, which had to be the English river to fit the text.

21. Gama: "Fathers Garnett and Oldecorne, guilty defendants of the gunpowder plot [*sic*]." The text and the poet's note have to do with the Gunpowder Plot of 1606. Gama omits the name of the conspirator who has become a folk figure; it is fair to imagine that the poet had never heard of Guy Fawkes. In addition, his accusations were directed at the Jesuits, not at a commoner executed as a result of a plot to blow up the Houses of Parliament. For a rebuttal, see the *Resposta Apologética*, p. 281.

   Burton, note intended. The numbers for Burton's proposed notes go from 18 here to 20 (line 83). In the transcription of the manuscript one number was skipped.

22. The reference (73-81) is to D. Sebastião, the last king of the Avis dynasty. Sebastian, a childless monarch, died at the age of twenty-four. A fanatic who fancied himself a man with a sacred mission, he decided to reconquer Portugal's former outposts in North Africa. In 1573, at nineteen, he led an unsuccessful expedition. Five years later, with a poorly organized army—and against advice from all sources—he met complete defeat and death at Alcacer-Kebir. Two years later Philip II of Spain took the Portuguese throne, and Portugal was under Spanish rule for six decades, until 1640. Some scholars say that it took more than a century for Portugal to recover from the defeat; there are those who think that Portugal never recovered and that 1578 was the end of the great era.

   In an unnecessary but reasonable rebuttal, the *Resposta Apologética* states that the king's death was not caused by the Society of Jesus (p. 253). It might be added here that the Society of Jesus, founded by Ignatius Loyola in 1540 with the main purpose of winning Protestants back to the Catholic Church, would have been in no position to interfere in the affairs of state in 1578.

Gama's charge becomes especially empty when we consider that King Sebastian was well known for making his own mistakes without the benefit of advice from others. It would also be inaccurate to describe Philip II of Spain as a tool of the Jesuits. One fact behind the text is the Spanish origin of the society, which Gama uses as a negative trait to be added to the others he has stated or implied. The passage and especially the note were written more for Pombal than for the general reader of the text.

23. Burton, note intended.
24. Gama: "See the *Dedução Cronológica,* a work which will serve as a landmark in the restoration of letters in Portugal: a monument of fervor, and of fidelity."

    The reference is to José Seabra da Silva, *Dedução Cronológica e Analítica* (Lisbon: Miguel Menescal, 1767). The first part is entitled *Parte Primeira. Na qual se manifesta pela sucessiva série de cada um dos reinados da Monarquia Portuguesa, que decorreram desde o governo do Senhor Rei D. João III até o presente, os horrorosos estragos, que a companhia denominada de Jesus fez em Portugal e em todos seus domínios, por um plano e sistema por ela inalteravelmente seguido desde que entrou neste Reino, até que foi dele proscrita e expulsa, pela justa, sábia e providente lei de 3 de setembro de 1759.* The second part has an equally lengthy and tendentious title. It is almost generally believed that Pombal was the real author of the tract, or at least that the book was written under his supervision.
25. Burton, note intended.
26. The original has *padres.* "Shepherd" was Burton's contribution, and the "flock" he added (line 110) completes the metaphor.
27. Burton omits line 109 of the original: "Que mansamente do lugar fugiam" (Who meekly from the place were fleeing).
28. Burton, note intended.
29. Tedeu. See note to IV. 113.
30. Burton, note intended. The number of his notes goes from 23 (line 124) to 25 (line 146), with one number skipped in the transcription of the text.
31. See note to IV. 131.
32. Burton concludes chapter 13 of his *Exploration of the Highlands of the Brazil* with a translation of the final lines of *O Uraguai* (V. 140-150), containing several minor differences from the rendition given here; see I. 143-144. These lines are, in a way, a repetition of IV. 84-89.
33. There has been some speculation regarding this person. See Introduction under the heading "The Poet," and Mário Camarinha da Silva, *O Uraguai,* p. 98; Antônio Cândido, *Vários Escritos,* pp.

164-165. In *The Exploration of the Highlands of the Brazil,* Burton states that Mireo was Gama's "poetical or pastoral name" (I.144), but in the biography that accompanies his translation, Sir Richard gives the correct "pastoral name," Termindo Sipílio. In the original, the name is pronounced in two syllables; Burton scans it as "Mi-re-o." Burton, note intended.

NOTES TO THE
BIOGRAPHICAL
NOTICE
[BURTON]

1. An opening note by Burton states that the essay is derived from the following sources: Ferdinand Denis, *Résumé d'histoire littéraire du Portugal suivi du résumé d'histoire littéraire du Brésil;* a life of José Basílio da Gama in the *Revista do Instituto Histórico e Geográfico Brasileiro;* Januário da Cunha Barbosa, *Parnaso Brasileiro;* Ferdinand Wolf, *Le Brésil littéraire;* Almeida Garrett, *Bosquejo de História da Poesia;* Pereira da Silva, *Plutarco Brasileiro;* Varnhagen, *História Geral do Brasil* and *Épicos Brasileiros.* For more information on these titles, see the Bibliography.
2. *Camoens: His Life and His Lusiads.* Burton worked on this book and the rest of his Camonian project during his stay in Brazil.
3. "The 'Chief Captains' who in the old Colonial days were appointed to command the different districts of Brazil." [Burton]
4. The currently accepted date is 1741. See, for example, Peixoto, "Nota Preliminar," *O Uraguai* (commemorative edition), p. viii, and Martins, *História da Inteligência Brasileira* 1:427.
5. Today Tiradentes, from the nickname of Joaquim José da Silva Xavier, a leader of the *Inconfidência Mineira* (1789), a conspiracy that aimed at independence, proclamation of a republic, and abolition of slavery. In *The Highlands of the Brazil* Burton mentions a visit to the village, "where there are seven churches," adding that "there is not a slab to honor the greatest of Brazilian poets" (1:143). He also recollected that "the beds of São José were not downy" (1:145).
6. Or twelve. See n. 4.
7. I. 98-103.
8. Probably 3 September 1758 and 19 January 1759. See Peixoto, "Nota Preliminar," *O Uraguai,* p. viii.
9. "This Viceroy was an exception to the rule of his fellows, he was a friend to the fine arts and he built the present Imperial Palace. Varnhagen [blank space] has attested to his character carefully and artistically." [Burton]
10. Probably *Minerva Brasiliense. Biblioteca Brasilica....* See Bibliography, "Editions of *O Uraguai,*" for complete lists.
11. The Jesuits.

12. A prestigious literary society founded in Rome in 1690. One of its objectives was the cultivation of pastoral poetry, reflected in its title and in the classical names adopted by its members.

13. Burton was British consul in Fernando Po from 1861 to 1864. He described his post as a "governmental crumb." Letter to Monckton Milnes, Lord Houghton, 20 March 1861, from the Lord Houghton Papers, Trinity College, Cambridge.

14. *Epitalâmio da Excelentíssima Senhora Maria Amália por José Basílio da Gama na Arcádia de Roma Termindo Sipílio.* Burton had found the text in the *Parnaso Brasileiro,* according to his note related to this passage.

15. Burton's manuscript includes partial translations of several poems, and also the Portuguese texts of the same passages. In the remainder of the "Biographical Notice," ellipses indicate places where other such translations occur.

16. *Quitúbia* (Lisbon: Antônio Rodrigues Galhardo, 1791). The plot of the poem does not actually deal with the Dutch invasion. Burton was misled by his source, Pereira da Silva, *Os Varões Ilustres,* 1:145.

17. *Os Campos Elíseos, Oitavas de Termindo Sipílio* (Lisbon: Régia Oficina Tipográfica, 1776).

18. The document was actually a brief entitled *Dominus ac Redemptor Noster.* Rev. Francis Xavier Talbot, "Society of Jesus," *Encyclopaedia Britannica.*

19. A group of five shields that form the national seal of Portugal.

20. Lugano: n.p., 1786. The notes that accompany the present edition of the poem have several references to this book, in the passages where the tract responds to charges by José Basílio da Gama, "M. Ferd. Denis tells us that it [Kaulen's book] contains at the end a curious map of the Missions." [Burton]. Denis was the author of *Résumé de l'histoire littéraire du Portugal suivi du résumé de l'histoire littéraire du Brésil.* See Bibliography.

21. Several words and groups of words are crossed out in the manuscript version of this sentence (*diabolical,* for example). The strongly anti-Jesuitical tone might lead one to suspect the censorship of Lady Burton.

22. D. José de Castro.

23. Gonzaga's poetic name is still remembered because his collection of lyric poems, which speak of an idealized woman whom he called Marília, had a title that combined two names: *Marília de Dirceu.* The book has been popular since the first printing in 1792. The popularity of the collection can be dramatized by the fact that in Rio de Janeiro there is a Marília de Dirceu Street.

24. Igreja da Boa Hora.

NOTES TO
THE NOTICE OF
THE URUGUAY
[BURTON]

1. "... The author would show that the Jesuits had established a despotic theocracy—the most abominable of tyrannies—in the New World. Startled by reports of a sprawling civilization springing up in the prairies and forests, Europe stood for a time with open mouth and José Basílio had the courage to rend the veil of Lies." [Burton]
2. See Burton's Preface.
3. "His action has the merit of extreme simplicity—it is natural as the conduct of his savages." [Burton]
4. Burton does not identify this line.
5. "*Os Varões Ilustres*, p. 377." [Burton]
6. Burton's quotation is from Almeida Garrett, *Bosquejo da Poesia Portuguesa*, p. 31. See Bibliography for additional information on this work.
7. In a marginal note Burton writes, "And José Basílio has at least as much local colour as Fenimore Cooper."
8. Thomas Welde of Roxbury (1595-1660/1661) was associate minister of the church in Roxbury. Along with his associate minister John Eliot (1596-1669) and Richard Mather (1596-1669), minister of Dorchester, he played an important role in bringing out the first edition of *The Bay Psalm Book* (1640). The verses cited by Burton are from the beginning of Psalm 137. Reprinted in the facsimile edition of *The Bay Psalm Book* (Chicago: University of Chicago Press, 1956), n.p.
9. Colonial American poet who lived 1631-1705.
10. Timothy Dwight (1752-1817). Grandson of Jonathan Edwards, and president of Yale University (1795-1817).
11. 1754-1812.
12. This paragraph, with slight variations, was used by Burton in "Translations," *The Athenaeum*, no. 2313 (24 February 1872), p. 242.
13. The first allusion is to the *Aeneid*, VI. 883, part of a series of predictions about the younger Marcellus. The Camonian reference is to *Os Lusíadas*, III. 118-135. Burton would publish a pamphlet

for private circulation entitled *Episode of Dona Inês de Castro* (London: Harrison and Son, 1879).

14. Ferdinand Wolf, author of *Le Brésil littéraire*. See Bibliography.

15. Underlined in the manuscript.

16. Burton's rendering of these lines is slightly different in the final version of the poem. In a marginal note he states: "For my part I have attempted to fulfil the prophecy and I hail with pleasure the opportunity of introducing this remarkable work to my countrymen." For another slight variation, see *The Highlands of the Brazil* 1:143-144.

17. See Bibliography.

18. This version was actually published in 1855. See Bibliography.

19. José de Alencar (1829-1877), novelist and exponent of Indianism. Burton translated one of his novels. See Introduction under the heading "The Translator."

20. For a discussion of the problems involved in dating Burton's manuscript, see Introduction under the heading "The Manuscript and Two Mysteries." The last two pages of the manuscript (pp. 97-98) contain a mélange of commentary and quotations from José de Santa Rita Durão and Coleridge, and historical notes that largely repeat what has been said in the Preface and beginning of the Notice.

O URAGUAY

O URAGUAY
POEMA
DE
JOSÉ BASILIO DA GAMA
NA ARCADIA DE ROMA
TERMINDO SIPILIO
DEDICADO
AO ILL.ᴹᴼ E EXC.ᴹᴼ SENHOR
FRANCISCO XAVIER
DE MENDONÇA FURTADO
SECRETARIO DE ESTADO
DE
S. MAGESTADE FIDELISSIMA
&c. &c. &c.

LISBOA
NA REGIA OFFICINA TYPOGRAFICA
ANNO MDCCLXIX
Com licença da Real Meza Cenſoria.

At ſpecus, & Caci detecta apparuit ingens
Regia, & umbroſae penitus patuere cavernae.

Virg. Æneid. Lib. VIII.

AO ILLUSTRISSIMO
E
EXCELLENTISSIMO SENHOR
CONDE DE OEYRAS

SONETO

*E*Rgue de jaspe hum globo alvo, e rotundo,
E em sima a estatua de hum Heroe perfeito;
Mas não lhe lavres nome em campo estreito,
Que o seu nome enche a terra, e o mar profundo.

Mostra no jaspe, Artifice facundo,
Em muda historia tanto illustre feito,
Paz, Justiça, Abundancia, e firme peito,
Isto nos basta a nós, e ao nosso Mundo.

Mas porque póde em seculo futuro,
Peregrino, que o mar de nós affasta,
Duvidar quem anima o jaspe duro,

Mostra-lhe mais Lisboa rica, e vasta,
E o Commercio, e em lugar remoto, e escuro,
Chorando a Hypocrisia. Isto lhe basta.

Do Author.

- - - - - saevis - - - - periclis
Servati facimus.
Virg. Æn. viii.

CANTO PRIMEIRO

FUMÃO ainda nas defertas praias
Lagos de fangue tepidos, e impuros,
Em que ondeão cadaveres defpidos,
Pafto de corvos. Dura inda nos valles
O rouco fom da irada artilheria.
Musa, honremos o Heroe, que o povo rude
Subjugou do Uraguay, e no feu fangue
Dos decretos reaes lavou a affronta.

Ai

Ai tanto cuſtas, ambição de imperio!

E Vós, por quem o Maranhão pendura

Rotas cadeias, e grilhões pezados,

Heroe, e Irmão de Heroes, ſaudoſa, e triſte,

Se ao longe a voſſa America vos lembra,

Protegei os meus verſos. Poſſa em tanto

Acoſtumar ao voo as novas azas,

Em que hum dia vos leve. Deſta ſorte

Medroſa deixa o ninho a vez primeira

Aguia, que depois foge á humilde terra,

E

E Vós. O Illuſtriſſimo, e Excellentiſſimo Senhor Franciſco Xavier de Mendonça Furtado foi Governador, e Capitão General das Gapitanias do Grão Pará, e Maranhão: e fez ao Norte do Brazil o que o Conde de Bobadela fez da parte do Sul: encontrou nos Jeſuitas a meſma reſiſtencia, e venceo-a da meſma ſorte.

Rotas cadeias. Os Indios lhe devem inteiramente a ſua liberdade. Os Jeſuitas nunca declamárão contra o cativeiro deſtes miſeraveis racionaes, ſenão porque portendião ſer ſó elles os ſeus Senhores. Ultimamente forão, nos noſſos dias, nobilitados, e admittidos aos cargos da Republica. Eſte procedimento honra a humanidade.

E vai ver de mais perto no ar vafio

O efpaço azul, onde não chega o raio.

Já dos olhos o véo tinha rafgado

A enganada Madrid, e ao novo Mundo

Da vontade do Rei nuncio fevero

Aportava Cataneo: e ao grande Andrade

Avifa que tem promptos os foccorros,

E que em breve fahia ao campo armado.

Não podia marchar por hum deferto

O

Irmão de Heroes. Em huma fó Familia achou o Rei tres Irmãos dignos de repartirem entre fi todo o pezo do Governo. Com quanto maior gloria noffa podem os eftranhos dizer da Corte de Lisboa, o que já fe diffe de Roma, ao vella nas mãos dos tres famofos Horacios, *Corneil. Horac.*:

E fon illuflre ardeur d' ofer plus que les autres
D' une feule maifon brave toutes les notres.
Ce choix pouvoit combler trois familles de gloire.

A enganada Madrid. Os Jefuitas por fi, e pelos feus fautores tinhão feito na Corte de Madrid o ultimo esforço para impedir a execução do Tratado de Limites.

Andrade. O Illuftriffimo, e Excellentiffimo Senhor Gomes Freire de Andrade.

O noſſo General, ſem que chegaſſem
As conducções, que ha muito tempo eſpera.
Já por dilatadiſſimos caminhos
Tinha mandado de remotas partes
Conduzir os petrechos para a guerra.
Mas entre tanto cuidadoſo, e triſte
Muitas couſas a hum tempo revolvia
No inquieto agitado penſamento.
Quando pelos ſeus guardas conduzido
Hum Indio, com inſignias de Correio,
Com ceremonia eſtranha lhe apreſenta
Humilde as cartas, que primeiro toca
Levemente na boca, e na cabeça.
Conhece a fiel mão, e já deſcança
O illuſtre General, que vio, raſgando,
Que na cera encarnada impreſſa vinha
A Aguia Real do generoſo Almeida.

                              Diz-

Almeida. O Coronel José Ignacio de Almeida.

Diz-lhe, que eſtá vizinho, e traz comſigo

Promptos para o caminho, e para a guerra

Os fogoſos cavallos, e os robuſtos,

E tardos bois, que hão de ſoffrer o jugo

No pezado exercicio das carretas.

Não tem mais que eſperar, e ſem demora

Reſponde ao Caſtelhano, que pártia,

E lhe determinou lugar, e tempo

Para unir os ſoccorros ao ſeu campo.

Juntos em fim, e hum corpo do outro á viſta,

Fez desfilar as Tropas pelo plano,

Porque viſſe o Heſpanhol em campo largo

A nobre gente, e as armas, que trazia.

Vão paſſando as eſquadras: elle em tanto

Tudo nota de parte, e tudo obſerva

Encoſtado ao baſtão. Ligeira, e leve

Paſſou primeiro a guarda, que na guerra

He

Lugar, e tempo. O dia 16 de Janeiro de 1756 em
Santo Antonio o Velho.

He primeira a marchar, e que a feu cargo

Tem defcubrir, e fegurar o campo.

Depois defta fe fegue a que defcreve,

E dá ao campo a ordem, e a figura,

E tranfporta, e edifica em hum momento

O leve tecto, e as movediças cafas,

E a Praça, e as ruas da Cidade errante.

Atrás dos forçofiffimos cavallos

Quentes fonoros eixos vão gemendo

Co' pezo da funefta artilheria.

Vinha logo de guardas rodeado,

Fonte de crimes, militar thefouro,

Por quem deixa no rego o curvo arado

O Lavrador, que não conhece a gloria;

E vendendo a vil preço o fangue, e a vida,

Move, e nem fabe porque move a guerra.

Intrepidos, e immoveis nas fileiras,

Com grandes paffos, firme a tefta, e os olhos,

Vão

Vão marchando os mitrados Granadeiros,

Sobre ligeiras rodas conduzindo

Novas efpecies de fundidos bronzes,

Que amiudão de promptas mãos fervidos,

E multiplicão pelo campo a morte.

Quem he efte, Cataneo perguntava,

Das brancas plumas, e de azul, e branco

Veftido, e de galões cuberto, e cheio,

Que traz a rica cruz no largo peito?

Gerardo, que os conhece, lhe refponde:

He o illuftre Menezes, mais que todos

Forte de braço, e forte de confelho.

Toda effa guerreira Infanteria,

A flor da mocidade, e da nobreza,

Como elle, azul, e branco, e ouro veftem.

Quem

Novas efpecies. As Companhias de Granadeiros le-
várão a efta expedição peças de amiudár, que fo-
rão as primeiras, que pafsárão ao Brazil.

Menezes. O Coronel Francifco Antonio Cardofo
de Menezes, hoje Governador da Colonia.

Quem he, continuava o Caſtelhano,

Aquelle velho vigoroſo, e forte,

Que de branco, e amarelo, e de ouro ornado

Vem os ſeus artilhéiros conduzindo?

Vês o grande Alpoim. Eſte o primeiro

Enſinou entre nós, por que caminho

Se eleva aos Ceos a curva, e grave bomba

Prenhe de fogo : e com que força do alto

Abate os tectos da Cidade, e lança

Do roto ſeio envolta em fumo a morte.

Seguião juntos o paterno exemplo

Dignos do grande Pai ambos os filhos.

Juſtos Ceos! E he forçoſo, illuſtre Vaſco,

Que te preparem as ſoberbas ondas,

                                    Lon-

Alpoim. O Brigadeiro.

Vaſco Fernandes Pinto Alpoim , filho do Briga-
deiro , e particular amigo do Author , morreo Te-
nente Coronel na flor dos ſeus annos em huma em-
barcação, que ſe perdeo, vindo da Colonia para o
Rio de Janeiro.

Longe de mim, a morte, e a fepultura?

Ninfas do mar, que viftes, fe he que viftes,

O rofto efmorecido, e os frios braços,

Sobre os olhos foltai as verdes tranças.

Trifte objecto de mágoa, e de faudade,

Como em meu coração, vive em meus verfos.

Com os teus encarnados Granadeiros

Tambem te vio naquelle dia o campo,

Famofo Mafcarenhas, tu, que agora

Em doce paz, nos menos firmes annos,

Igualmente fervindo ao Rei, e á Patria,

Dictas as Leis ao público focego,

Honra da Toga, e gloria do Senado.

Nem tu, Caftro fortiffimo, efcolhefte

O

Mafcarenhas. Fernando Mafcarenhas, Capitão de Granadeiros, depois Sargento mór, actualmente ferve no Senado.

Caftro. O Tenente Coronel Gregorio de Caftro Moraes de illuftriffima Familia, que teve o governo do Rio de Janeiro no tempo da invasão do famofo Du Guay Trouin.

O defcanço da Patria : o campo, e as armas
Fizeráo renovar no inclyto peito
Todo o heroico valor dos teus paffados.

Os ultimos, que em campo fe moftráráo,
Foráo fortes dragóes de duros peitos,
Promptos para dous generos de guerra,
Que pelejáo a pé fobre as montanhas,
Quando o pede o terreno; e quando o pede,
Erguem nuvens de pó por todo o campo
Co' tropel dos magnanimos cavallos.

Convida o General depois da moftra,
Pago da militar guerreira imagem
Os feus, e os Hefpanhoes, e já recebe
No pavilháo purpureo, em largo gyro,
Os Capitáes a alegre, e rica meza.
Defterráo-fe os cuidados, derramando
Os vinhos Europeos nas taças de ouro.
Ao fom da eburnea cythara fonora

Ar-

Arrebatado de furor divino

Do feu Heroe Matufio celebrava

Altas emprezas dignas de memoria.

Honras futuras lhe promette, e canta

Os feus brazões, e fobre o forte efcudo

Já de então lhe afigura, e lhe defcreve

As perolas, e o titulo de Grande.

Levantadas as mezas, entretinháo

O congreffo de Heroes difcurfos varios.

Alli Cataneo ao General pedia,

Que do principio lhe diffeffe as caufas

Da nova guerra, e do fatal tumulto.

Se aos Padres feguem os rebeldes póvos?

Quem os governa em paz, e na peleja?

Que do premeditado occulto Imperio

Vagamente na Europa fe fallava.

B   Nos

Vagamente. Os Jefuitas tem tido a animofidade
de negàr por toda Europa o que fe acabou de paffar
na America nos noffos dias á vifta de dous Exercitos.

Nos seus lugares cada qual immovel

Pende da sua boca : attende em roda

Tudo em silencio, e dá principio Andrade.

O nosso ultimo Rei, e o Rei de Hespanha

Determinárão, por cortar de hum golpe,

Como sabeis, neste angulo da terra,

As desordens de póvos confinantes,

Que mais certos sinaes nos dividissem.

Tirando a linha, de onde a esteril costa,

E

O Author o experimentou em Roma, onde muitas pessoas o buscavão só para saberem com fundamento as noticias do Uraguay : testemunhando hum estranho contentamento de encontrarem hum Americano, que os podia informar miudamente de tudo o succedido. A admiração, que causava a estranheza de factos entre nós tão conhecidos, fez nascer as primeiras idéas deste Poema.

Mais certos sinaes. O Tratado de Limites das Conquistas celebrou-se a 16 de Janeiro de 1750 entre os Senhores Reis D. João o V de Portugal, e D. Fernando o VI de Hespanha. Este Tratado feria os Jesuitas na alma, porque por elle se entregavão aos Portuguezes as terras, que a Companhia depois de muito-tempo possuia como suas da parte Oriental do Rio Uraguay.

E o cerro de Caftilhos o mar lava

Ao monte mais vizinho, e que as vertentes

Os termos do dominio affinalaffem.

Voffa fica a Colonia, e ficão noffos

Sete póvos, que os Barbaros habitão

Naquella Oriental vafta campina,

Que o fertil Uraguay difcorre, e banha.

Quem podia efperar que huns Indios rudes,

Sem difciplina, fem valor, fem armas,

Se atraveffaffem no caminho aos noffos,

E que lhes difputaffem o terreno!

Em fim não lhes dei ordens para a guerra:

Fruftrada a expedição, em fim voltárão.

C'o voffo General me determino

A entrar no campo juntos, em chegando

B ii A

Sem difciplina. Como naquelle tempo fe imaginava.
Lhes difputaffem. Os Officiaes Militares, que forão
fazer a demarcação, chegárão ao pofto de Santa Te-
cla, e nelle achárão fortificados os Indios, que lhes
impedirão os paffos.

A doce volta da eſtação das flores.

Não ſoffrem tanto os Indios atrevidos:

Juntos hum noſſo forte em tanto aſſaltão:

E os Padres os incitão, e acompanhão.

Que, á ſua diſcrição, ſó elles podem

Aqui mover, ou ſocegar a guerra.

Os Indios, que ficárão prizioneiros,

Ainda os podeis ver neſte meu campo.

Deixados os quarteis, em fim partimos

Por

Prizioneiros. Forão ſincoenta eſtes prizioneiros: alguns dos princípaes vierão remettidos ao Rio de Janeiro, onde o Author os vio, e fallou com elles. Conſeſſavão ingenuamente, que os Padres tinhão vindo em ſua companhia até o Rio Pardo, e ſe tinhão deixado ficar da outra banda. Moſtravão-ſe ſurprendidos da doçura, que encontravão no trato dos Portuguezes. Dizião que os Padres não ceſſavão de lhes intimar nas ſuas prégaçóes, que os Portuguezes tinhão o diabo no corpo, e que erão todos ſeiticeiros. Que em matando algum, para que não tornaſſe a viver, era neceſſario pòr-lhe a cabeça hum palmo longe do corpo: o que elles religioſamente obſervavão.

Partimos. Sahio o General Portuguez do Rio Grande de S. Pedro a 28 de Julho de 1754.

Por diverſas eſtradas, procurando

Tomar no meio os rebelados póvos.

Por muitas leguas de aſpero caminho,

Por lagos, boſques, valles, e montanhas,

Chegámos onde nos impede o paſſo

Arrebatado, e caudaloſo rio.

Por toda a oppoſta margem ſe deſcobre

De Barbaros o numero infinito,

Que ao longe nos inſulta, e nos eſpera.

Preparo curvas balſas, e pelotas,

E em huma parte de paſſar aceno,

                                        Em

Caudaloſo rio. Jacui. Chegárão a elle aos 7 de Se-
tembro.

Balſas, e pelotas. Eſpecie de barcos, em que os
noſſos paſsão naquelle paiz os maiores, e mais pro-
fundos rios. Fazem-ſe de couros de boi. Levão no
fundo as cargas, e em ſima os homens com os ca-
vallos nadando á mão. Os Indios, que ſão robuſtiſ-
ſimos, e grandes nadadores, tirão toda eſta maqui-
na por huma corda, cuja ponta toinão nos dentes.
Quem vai dentro leva na mão a outra ponta, lar-
gando-a mais, ou menos, conforme julga ſer neceſ-
ſario.

Em quanto em outra paſſo occulto as Tropas.

Quaſi tocava o fim da empreza, quando

Do voſſo General hum menſageiro

Me affirma, que ſe havia retirado.

A diſciplina militar dos Indios

Tinha eſterilizado aquelles campos.

Que eu tambem me retire me aconſelha,

Até que o tempo moſtre outro caminho.

Irado, não o nego, lhe reſpondo:

Que para traz não ſei mover hum paſſo.

Venha quando puder, que eu firme o eſpero.

Porém o Rio, e a fórma do terreno

Nos

Se havia retirado. Retirárão-ſe as Tropas Caſtelha-
nas, enfraquecida a Cavallcria. Tinhão-ſe mettido
muito pela margem do rio, que eſtava rapada dos
gados Jeſuiticos. Finalmente não tinhão vontade de
entrar em Miſsões: nem até então eſtavão inteira-
mente perſuadidos da intenção do Rei. A maior ra-
zão de duvidar naſcia das cartas, que vinhão da Cor-
te de Madrid por huma occulta cabala; os Jeſuitas
tudo revolvião, e maquinavão mais que nunca.

Fórma do terreno. Todos aquelles boſques, e var-
geas por muitas, e muitas leguas são alagadiços, e

Nos faz não vista, e nunca usada guerra.

Sahe furioso do seu seio, e toda

Vai alagando com o desmedido

Pezo das aguas a planicie immensa.

As tendas levantei, primeiro aos troncos;

Depois aos altos ramos: pouco a pouco

Fomos tomar na região do vento

A habitação aos leves passarinhos.

Tece o emaranhadissimo arvoredo

Verdes, irregulares, e torcidas

Ruas, e praças de huma, e de outra ban-
da;

Cru-

sujeitos a estas enchentes. Ha Nações inteiras de In-
dios, que fazem as suas choupanas, e vivem sobre
as arvores. São destrissimos em subir, e descer sem
cordas, nem genero algum de escada. As arvores são
altissimas, e tem a maior parte do anno as raizes
na agua.

As tendas. Talvez não se achará na Historia outro
successo semelhante. Foi necessaria toda a constancia
do Conde de Bobadela para ter dous mezes hum Ex-
ercito abarracado sobre as arvores.

Cruzadas de canoas. Taes podemos
Co'a miſtura das luzes, e das ſombras
Ver por meio de hum vidro tranſplantados
Ao ſeio de Adria os nobres edificios,
E os jardins, que produz outro elemento.

E batidas do remo, e navegaveis
As ruas da maritima Veneza.

Duas vezes a Lua prateada
Curvou no Ceo ſereno os alvos cornos,
E inda continuava a groſſa enchente.

Tudo nos falta no paiz deſerto.
Tardar devia o Heſpanhol ſoccorro.
E de ſi nos lançava o rio, e o tempo.
Cedí, e retirei-me ás noſſas terras.
Deo fim á narração o invicto Andrade,

E

Canoas. Pequenas embarcações dos Indios feitas
de hum ſó tronco : nellas vinhão occultamente fa-
zer commercio com os Portuguezes, e Heſpanhoes.
Tardar devia. *Poſt bellum auxilium.*

E antes de fe foltar o ajuntamento,
Com os regios poderes, que occultára,
Sorprende os feus, e os animos alegra,
Enchendo os poftos todos do feu campo.
O corpo de Dragões a Almeida entrega,
E campo das mercês o lugar chama.

FIM DO PRIMEIRO CANTO.

CAN-

CANTO SEGUNDO

Depois de haver marchado muitos dias,
Em fim junto a hum ribeiro, que atravessa
Sereno, e manso hum curvo, e fresco valle,
Achárão, os que o campo descubrião,
Hum cavallo anhelante, e o peito, e as ancas
Cuberto de suor, e branca escuma.
Temos perto o inimigo: aos seus dizia
O esperto General: sei que costumão
Trazer os Indios hum voluvel laço,

Com

Com o qual tomáo no efpaçofo campo
Os cavallos, que encontráo; e rendidos
Aqui, e alli com o continuado
Galopear, a quem primeiro os fegue
Deixáo os feus, que em tanto fe reftauráo.

Nem fe enganou; porque ao terceiro dia
Formados os achou fobre huma larga
Ventajofa colina, que de hum lado
He cuberta de hum bofque, e do outro lado
Corre efcarpada, e fobranceira a hum rio.

Notava o General o fitio forte,
Quando Menezes, que vizinho eftava,
Lhe diz: Neftes defertos encontramos
Mais do que fe efperava, e me parece
Que fó por força d'armas poderemos
Inteiramente fujeitar os póvos.

Torna-lhe o General: Tentem-fe os meios
De

Ao terceiro dia. Aos 10 de Fevereiro de 1756.

De brandura, e de amor; se isto não basta,

Farei a meu pezar o ultimo esforço.

Mandou, dizendo assim, que os Indios todos,

Que tinha prizioneiros no seu campo,

Fossem vestidos das formosas cores,

Que a inculta gente simples tanto adora.

Abraçou-os a todos, como filhos,

E deo a todos liberdade. Alegres

Vão buscar os parentes, e os amigos,

E a huns, e a outros contão a grandeza

Do excelso coração, e peito nobre

Do General famoso, invicto Andrade.

Já para o nosso campo vem descendo,

Por mandado dos seus, dous dos mais nobres,

Sem arcos, sem aljavas; mas as testas

De varias, e altas penas coroadas,

E cercadas de penas as cinturas,

E os pés, e os braços, e o pescoço. Entrára
                                    Sem

Sem moftras, nem final de cortezia,

Cepé no pavilhão. Porém Cacambo

Fez, ao feu modo, cortezia eftranha,

E começou: Ó General famofo,

Tu tens á vifta quánta gente bebe

Do foberbo Uraguay a efquerda margem.

Bem que os noffos Avôs foffem defpojo
                                        Da

E começou. Todos os Padres aprendião a lingua
dos Indios, e prohibião a eftes, contra a intenção
do Rei, ufar de outra lingua, que não foffe a fua
nacional. Defta forte ficava impoffibilitada a communicação com os Portuguezes, e Caftelhanos, e impenetravel o fegredo do que fe paffava naquelles certões. E o que he mais, he que os mefmos Jefuitas
fe jactavão defta efpecie de tyrannia na face de toda Europa:

  Nefcia gens noftri vivit - - - - - - -
   - - - - - ad interiora venire
 Regna vetent homines cupidos audita videndi.
     Vanier. Praed. ruft. Lio. XIV.

 *Noffos Avôs. Por eftes Portuguezes fe nos trazem a
cafa todos os prefentes prejuizos. Lembrai-vos que nos
tempos paffados matárão a voffos defuntos Avôs. Matárão mais milhares delles por todas as partes, fem refervar as innocentes creaturas.* Inftrucções, &c.

Da perfidia de Europa, e daqui mesmo

C'os não vingados ossos dos parentes

Se vejão branquejar ao longe os valles,

Eu desarmado, e só buscar-te venho.

Tanto espero de ti. E em quanto as armas

Dão lugar á razão, Senhor, vejamos

Se se póde salvar a vida, e o sangue

De tantos desgraçados. Muito tempo

Póde ainda tardar-nos o recurso

Com

Buscar-te venho. Tinhão positiva ordem dos Padres para o não fazerem. *Os que nos aborrecem,* (por estas expressões caracterizavão os Europeos) *quando nos pertendão fallar, havemos de escusar sua conversação, fugindo muito da dos Hespanhoes, e muito mais dos Portuguezes .... Se acaso nos quizerem fallar, hão de ser sinco Castelhanos, nada mais. Não sejão Portuguezes; porque se viessem alguns dos Portuguezes, não lhes ha de ir bem. O Padre, que he o dos Indios, e sabe a sua lingua, ha de ser o que sirva de interprete, e então se fará tudo, porque deste modo se fará tudo como Deos manda; e senão, irão as cousas por onde o Diabo quizer.* Instrucções, &c.

Tanto espero de ti. Não queremos ir aonde vós estais, porque não temos confiança de vós-outros. Instrucções.

Com o largo Oceano de permeio,
Em que os fufpiros dos vexados póvos
Perdem o alento. O dilatar-fe'a entrega
Eftá nas noffas máos, até que hum dia
Informados os Reis nos reftituáo
A doce antiga paz. Se o Rei de Hefpanha
Ao teu Rei quer dar terras com máo larga,
Que lhe dê Buenos Aires, e Correntes,
E outras, que tem por eftes vaftos climas;
Porém não póde dar-lhe os noffos póvos.
E inda no cafo que pudeffe dallos,
Eu não fei fe o teu Rei fabe o que troca;
Porém tenho receio que o não faiba.
Eu já ví a Colonia Portugueza
Na tenra idade dos primeiros annos,
Quando o meu velho pai c'os noffos arcos
Ás fitiadoras Tropas Caftelhánas
Deo foccorro, e medío comvofco as armas.

E

E quererão deixar os Portuguezes

A Praça, que avaſſalla, e que domina

O Gigante das aguas, e com ella

Toda a navegação do largo rio,

Que parece que poz a natureza

Para ſervir-vos de limite, e raia?

Será; mas não o creio. E depois diſto,

As campinas, que vês, e a noſſa terra,

Sem o noſſo ſuor, e os noſſos braços,

De que ſerve ao teu Rei? Aqui não temos

Nem altas minas, nem os caudaloſos

Rios de arêas de ouro. Eſſa riqueza,

C   Que

Aqui não temos. Os Padres fazião crer aos Indios que os Portuguezes erão gente ſem lei, que adora-vão o ouro.

Eſſa riqueza. As ſuas riquezas erão immenſas: as ſuas Caſas, e os ſeus Templos magnificos, fóra de quanto ſe póde imaginar em Europa. Nem he ne-ceſſario ir tão longe: meſino no Rio de Janeiro ti-não os Padres, entre outras immenſas terras, a fa-zenda de Santa Cruz; tão grande, que nenhuma da-quellas opulentiſſimas familias ſe achou até hoje com fundo para compralla. Tinhão ſó neſta mais de mil

Que cobre os templos dos bemditos Padres,

Fruto da sua industria, e do commercio

Da folha, e pelles, he riqueza sua.

Com o arbitrio dos corpos, e das almas

O Ceo lha deo em sorte. A nós somente

Nos toca arar, e cultivar a terra,

Sem

escravos. O gado era sem numero. Com tudo isto, he cousa certa que se lhes não achou dinheiro de consideração no seu sequestro. Poucos dias depois de partirem daquelle Porto se apresentou ao Conde de Bobadela hum Leigo pedreiro, dizendo, que vinha descubrir o lugar, onde por ordem dos Padres tinha escondido o dinheiro. Com effeito já se não achou mais que o lugar nos alicerces da Igreja nova. Elles assim que virão que o Leigo despia a roupeta, fizerão-lhe huma ligeireza das suas.

Da folha, e pelles. Os Indios, e os Hespanhoes fazem do *Mate* o uso, que os Chinezes fazem do seu *The.* Este importantissimo commercio era todo dos Jesuitas do Paraguay. Cultivavão as arvores, que dão a tal folha, e fabricavão-na, e a fazião gyrar em surrões de pelle por toda a America Hespanhola. Só este negocio rendia em cada hum anno muitos milhões. Tudo suor dos miseraveis Indios.

Riqueza sua. *Semina nos colimus faustis, quae jecimus agris.*
              Vanier. Praed. rust. Lib. xiv.

Sem outra paga mais que o repartido

Por máos efcaças mifero fuftento.

Pobres choupanas, e algodóes tecidos,

E o arco, e as fettas, e as viftofas penas

São as noffas fantafticas riquezas.

Muito fuor, e pouco, ou nenhum fafto.

Volta, Senhor, não paffes adiante.

Que mais queres de nós? Não nos obrigues

C ii   A

Sem outra paga. - - - *proprium, qui nil potiuntur, & ufu*
        Cuncta tenent - - - - Ibid.

Muito fuor. Tambem não he neceffario ir ao Ura-
guay para ter provas do exceffivo trabalho dos In-
dios no ferviço dos Padres. Entre a Villa de Santos,
e a Cidade de S. Paulo ha huma ferra muito ingre-
me, e dilatada: não fe póde fubir a cavallo. O Con-
de de Bobadela, o melhor cavalleiro do feu tempo,
cahio duas vezes logo á entrada, em cavallos, que ti-
nha efcolhido para iffo entre muitos. Todos a fobem
a pé com o feu cavallo pela mão. Os Padres como
fazião voto de pobreza, contentavão-fe de a fubir,
e defcer recoftados em redes ás coftas dos miferaveis
Indios: nem já mais paffarão por alli de outra forte.
Efte facto na Europa parece incrivel; mas o Author
o attefta.

A refiftir-te em campo aberto. Póde
Cuftar-te muito fangue o dar hum paffo.
Não queiras ver fe cortão noffas frexas.
Vê que o nome dos Reis não nos affufta.
O teu eftá mui longe ; e nós os Indios
Não temos outro Rei mais do que os Padres.
Acabou de fallar ; e affim refponde
O illuftre General : Ó alma grande,
Digna de combater por melhor caufa,
Vê que te enganão : rifca da memoria
Vens, funeftas imagens, que alimentão
Envelhecidos mal fundados odios.
Por mim te falla o Rei : ouve-me, attende,
E verás huma vez nua a verdade.
Fez-vos livres o Ceo ; mas fe o fer livres
Era viver errantes, e difperfos,

Sem

O nome dos Reis. Eftas expreffóes não são ornato
da Poefia, paffou na realidade tudo o que o Author
aqui faz dizer a efte Indio.

Sem companheiros, fem amigos, fempre
Com as armas na mão em dura guerra,
Ter por juftiça a força, e pelos bofques
Viver do acafo, eu julgo que inda fora
Melhor a efcravidão, que a liberdade.

Mas nem a efcravidão, nem a miferia
Quer o benigno Rei que o fruto feja
Da fua protecção Effe abfoluto
Imperio illimitado, que exercitão
Em vós os Padres, como vós, vaffallos,
He imperio tyrannico, que ufurpão.

Nem são Senhores, nem vós fois Efcravos.
O Rei he voffo Pai: quer-vos felices.
Sois livres, como eu fou; e fereis livres,
Não fendo aqui, em outra qualquer parte.
Mas deveis entregar-nos eftas terras.
Ao bem público cede o bem privado.
O focego de Europa affim o pede.

Affim

Aſſim o manda o Rei. Vós ſois rebeldes,
Senão obedeceis; mas os rebeldes,
Eu ſei que não ſois vós, ſáo os bons Padres,
Que vos dizem a todos, que ſois livres,
E ſe ſervem de vós, como de eſcravos.
Armados de orações vos póem no campo
Contra o fero trováo da artilheria,
Que os muros arrebata, e ſe contentáo
De ver de longe a guerra: ſacrificáo
Avarentos do ſeu o voſſo ſangue.
Eu quero á voſſa viſta deſpojallos
Do tyranno dominio deſtes climas,
De que a voſſa innocencia os fez ſenhores.
Dizem-vos que não tendes Rei? Cacique,
E o juramento de fidelidade?
Porque eſtá longe, julgas que não póde
Caſtigar-vos a vós, e caſtigallos?
Generoſo inimigo, he tudo engano.

Os

Os Reis eſtáo na Europa; mas adverte

Que eſtes braços que vês, são os ſeus braços.

Dentro de pouco tempo hum meu aceno

Vai cubrir eſte monte, e eſſas campinas

De ſemivivos palpitantes corpos

De miſeros mortaes, que inda não ſabem

Porque cauſa o ſeu ſangue vai agora

Lavar a terra, ę recolher-ſe em lagos.

Náo me chames cruel: em quanto he tempo

Penſa, e reſolve; e pela máo tomando

Ao nobre Embaixador o illuſtre Andrade,

Intenta reduzillo por brandura.

E o Indio, hum pouco penſativo, o braço,

E a máo retira; e ſuſpirando, diſſe:

Gentes de Europa, nunca vos trouxera

O mar, e o vento a nós. Ah! não de balde

Eſtendeo entre nós a natureza

Todo eſſe plano eſpaço immenſo de aguas.

Pro-

Proseguia talvez ; mas o interrompe

Cepé , que entra no meio , e diz : Cacambo

Fez mais do que devia ; e todos sabem

Que estas terras , que pizas , o Ceo livres

Deo aos nossos Avôs ; nós tambem livres

As recebemos dos antepassados.

Livres as háo de herdar os nossos filhos.

Desconhecemos , detestamos jugo ,

Que não seja o do Ceo , por máo dos Padres.

As frexas partirão nossas contendas

Dentro de pouco tempo ; e o vosso Mundo ,

Se nelle hum resto houver de humanidade ,

Jul-

---

*Estas terras. Estas terras no-las deo Deos , e a nos-
sos Avôs , e por isso só as possuimos em amor de Deos.*
Carta sediciosa , &c.

O do Ceo. Esta mistura do sagrado com o profa-
no , ou para melhor dizer , aquelle fazer servir a Re-
ligião aos seus fins particulares , foi sempre o ca-
racter dos Jesuitas. Considere-se attentamente este
verso :

Non gentem imperio , sed relligione tenemus.
                              Vanier. sup.

Julgará entre nós; se defendemos
Tu a injuſtiça, e nós o Deos, e a Patria.

Em fim quereis a guerra, e tereis guerra,
Lhe torna o General: podeis partir-vos,
Que tendes livre o paſſo. Aſſim dizendo,
Manda dar a Cacambo rica eſpada
De tortas guarnições de prata, e ouro,
A que inda mais valor dera o trabalho.
Hum bordado chapeo, e larga cinta
Verde, e capa de verde, e fino panno,
Com bandas amarelas, e encarnadas.

E mandou que a Cepé ſe déſſe hum arco
De pontas de marfim: e ornada, e cheia
De novas ſettas a famoſa aljava:
A meſma aljava, que deixára hum dia,
Quando envolto em ſeu ſangue, e vivo apenas,
Sem arco, e ſem cavallo, foi trazido
Prizioneiro de guerra ao noſſo campo.

Lem-

Lembrou-ſe o Indio da paſſada injuria,

E ſobraçando a conhecida aljava,

Lhe diſſe: Ó General, eu te agradeço

As ſettas, que me dás, e te prometto

Mandar-tas bem de preſſa huma por huma

Entre nuvens de pó no ardor da guerra.

Tu as conhecerás pelas feridas,

Ou porque rompem com mais força os arcs.

Deſpedírão-ſe os Indios, e as eſquadras

Se vão diſpondo em ordem de peleja,

Como mandava o General. Os lados

Cobrem as Tropas de Cavalleria,

E eſtão no centro firmes os Infantes.

Qual fera boca de Libreo raivoſo

De liſos, e alvos dentes guarnecida,

Os Indios ameaça a noſſa frente

De agudas baionetas rodeada.

Fez a trombeta o ſom da guerra. Ouvírão
Aquel-

Aquelles montes pela vez primeira
O fom da caixa Portugueza; e vírão
Pela primeira vez aquelles ares
Defenroladas as Reaes bandeiras.

Sahem das grutas pelo chão cavadas,
Em que até li de induſtria fe efcondião,
Nuvens de Indios, e a viſta duvidava
Se do terreno os barbaros nafcião.

Qual já no tempo antigo o errante Cadmo
Dizem que víra da fecunda terra
Brotar a crueliſſima feara.

Erguem todos hum barbaro alarido,
E fobre os noſſos cada qual encurva
Mil vezes, e mil vezes folta o arco
Hum chuveiro de fettas defpedindo.

Gentil Mancebo prefumido, e nefcio,
A quem a popular lifonja engana,
Vaidofo pelo campo difcorria,

Fa-

Fazendo oftentação dos feus penachos.

Impertinente, e de familia efcura,

Mas que tinha o favor dos fantos Padres.

Contão, não fei fe he certo, que o tivera

A efteril Mãi por orações de Balda.

Chamárão-#o Baldetta por memoria.

Tinha hum cavallo de manchada pelle

Mais viftofo que forte: a natureza

Hum ameno jardim por todo o corpo

Lhe debuxou, e era Jardim chamado.

O Padre na faudofa defpedida

Deo-lho em final de amor; e nelle agora

Gy-

Balda. O P. Lourenço Balda foi huma das cabeças mais tenazes , e que mais animava os Indios á rebelião.

Por memoria. Os Jefuitas da America não erão tão efcrupulofos como affectavão fer os da Europa. Era bem facil diftinguir nas Aldeas as Indias, que gozavão do favor dos Padres. Da mefma forte fe diftinguião muito bem, entre os outros, os rapazes da familia. Na Afia era o mefmo. Lea-fe a Carta do Bifpo de Nankim a Benedicto XIV.

Gyrando ao largo com incertos tiros
Muitos feria, e a todos inquietava.

Mas fe então fe cubrio de eterna infamia,
A gloria tua foi, nobre Gerardo.

Tornava o Indio jactanciofo, quandô
Lhe fahe Gerardo ao meio da carreira:
Difparou-lhe a piftola, e fez-lhe a hum tempo '
Co' reflexo do Sol luzir a efpada.

Só de vello fe affufta o Indio, e fica
Qual quem ouve o trovão, e efpera o raio.

Treme, e o cavallo aos feus volta, e pendente
A hum lado, 'e a outro de cahir acena.

Deixando aqui, e alli por todo o campo
Entornadas as fettas; pelas coftas,
Fluctuavão as penas; e fugindo
Soltas da mão as redeas ondeavão.

In-

Sinal de amor. - - - - - *quem candida Dido*
Effe fui dederat monumentum, & pignus amoris.
Virg. Æn. Lib. v.

Infta Gerardo, e quafi o ferro o alcança,

Quando Tatú Guaçú, o mais valente

De quantos Indios vło a noffa idade,

Armado o peito da efcamofa pelle

De hum'Jacaré disforme, que matára,

Se atraveffa diante. Intenta o noffo

Com a outra piftola abrir caminho,

E em vão o intenta : a verdenegra pelle,

Que ao Indio o largo peito orna, e defende,

Formou a natureza impenetravel.

Co' a efpada o fere no hombro, e na cabeça,

E as penas córta, de que o campo efpalha.

Separa os dous fortiffimos guerreiros

A

Tatú Guaçú. Guafú na lingua dos Indios quer dizer *grande.* Alguns Indios mais foberbos ajuntão efta palavra ao feu nome, que fica foando defta forte, entre elles, como foa, entre nós, Carlos Magno, Alexandre Magno, &c.

Jacaré. Com efte nome o traz Marcgr. Braf. 242. Veja-fe Linac. Syftem. Natur. Amphibia, Reptilia, Draco. 1.

A multidão dos nossos, que atropela
Os Indios fugitivos: tão de pressa
Cobrem o campo os mortos, e os feridos,
E por nós a victoria se declara.
Precipitadamente as armas deixão,
Nem resistem mais tempo ás espingardas.
Vale-lhe a costumada ligeireza,
De baixo lhe desapparece a terra,
E voão, que o temor aos pés póe azas,
Clamando ao Ceo, e encommendando a vida
Ás orações dos Padres. Desta sorte,
Talvez, em outro clima, quando soltão
A branca neve eterna os velhos Alpes,
Arrebata a corrente impetuosa
                                    Co'

Tão de pressa. Ainda que os Padres tinhão armado
os Indios, e feito quanto podião para os disciplinar,
com tudo estavão bem longe de poder resistir ás Tro-
pas regulares. Era necessaria muita crueldade para
entregar aquelles miseraveis á morte só por ambi-
ção, e por caprixo.

Co' as choupanas o gado. Afflicto, e trifte

Se falva o Lavrador nos altos ramos,

E vê levar-lhe a cheia os bois, e o arado.

Poucos Indios no campo mais famofos,

Servindo de reparo aos fugitivos,

Suftentão todo o pezo da batalha,

A pezar da fortuna. De huma parte

Tatú Guaçú mais forte na defgraça

Já banhado em feu fangue pertendia

Por feu braço elle fó pôr termo á guerra.

Caitutú de outra parte altivo, e forte

Oppunha o peito á furia do inimigo,

E fervia de muro á fua gente.

Fez proezas Cepé naquelle dia.

Conhecido de todos, no perigo

Moftrava defcuberto o rofto, e o peito

Forçando os feus co' exemplo, e co' as palavras.

Já tinha defpejado a aljava toda,

E

E deftro em atirar, e irado, e forte
Quantas fettas da máo voar fazia,
Tantas na noffa gente enfanguentava.
Settas de novo agora recebia,
Para dar outra vez principio á guerra.
Quando o illuftre Hefpanhol, que governava
Montevidio alegre, airofo, e prompto
As redeas volta ao rapido cavallo,
E por fima de mortos, e feridos,
Que luctaváo co' a morte, o Indio affronta.
Cepé, que o vio, tinha tomado a lança,
E atrás deitando a hum tempo o corpo, e o
        braço,
A defpedio. Por entre o braço, e o corpo
Ao lígeiro Hefpanhol q̃ ferro paffa:
Rompe, fem fazer damno, a terra dura,
E treme fóra muito. tempo a haftea.
Mas de hum golpe a Cepé na tefta, e peito

Fere o Governador, e as redeas córta

Ao cavallo feroz. Foge o cavallo,

E levá involuntario, e ardendo em ira

Por todo o campo a feu Senhor; e ou foffe

Que regada de fangue aos pés cedia

A terra, ou que puzeffe as máos em falfo,

Rodou fobre fi mefmo, e na cahida

Lançou longe a Cepé. Rende-te, ou morre,

Grita. o Governador; e o Tape altivo,

Sem refponder, encurva o arco, e a fetta

Defpede, e nella lhe prepara a morte.

Enganou-fe efta vez. A fetta hum pouco

Declina, e açouta o rofto a leve pluma.

Náo quiz deixar o vencimento incerto

Por mais tempo o Hefpanhol, e arrebatado

Com a piftola lhe fez tiro aos peitos.

Era pequeno o efpaço, e fez o tiro

No corpo defarmado eftrago horrendo.

Viáo-

Vião-ſe dentro pelas rotas coſtas
Palpitar as entranhas. Quiz tres vezes
Levantar-ſe do chão: cahio tres vezes,
E os olhos já nadando em fria morte
Lhe cubrio ſombra eſcura, ę ferreo ſono.
Morto o grande Cepé, já não reſiſtem
As timidas eſquadras. Não conhece
Leis o temor. De balde eſtá diante,
E anima os ſeus o rapido Cacambo.
Tinha-ſe retirado da peleja
Caitutú mal ferido; e do ſeu corpo
Deixa Tatú Guaçú por onde paſſa
Rios de ſangue. Os outros mais valentes
Ou erão mortos, ou feridos. Pende
O ferro vencedor ſobre os vencidos.
Ao numero, ao valor cede Cacambo:
Salva os Indios, que póde, e ſe retira.

FIM DO SEGUNDO CANTO.
D ii CAN-

CANTO TERCEIRO

JÁ a noſſa do Mundo ultima Parte
Tinha voltado a enſanguentada fronte
Ao centro luminar; quando a campanha
Semeada de mortos, e inſepultos
Vio desfazer-ſe a hum tempo a Villa errante
Ao ſom das caixas. Deſcontente, e triſte
Marchava o General: não ſoffre o peito
Compadecido, e generoſo a viſta

Da-

Voltado. He dito por hypotheſe.

Daquelles frios, e fangrados corpos,
Victimas da ambição de injufto imperio.
Forão ganhando, e defcubrindo terra
Inimiga, e infiel; até que hum dia
Fizerão alto, e fe acampárão, onde
Incultas vargeas, por efpaço immenfo,
Enfadonhas, e eftereis acompanhão
Ambas as margens de hum profundo rio.
Todas eftas vaftiffimas campinas
Cobrem paluftres, e tecidas canas,
E leves juncos do calor toftados,
Prompta materia de voraz incendio.
O Indio habitador de quando em quando
Com eftranha cultura entrega ao fogo
Muitas leguas de campo: o incendio dura,
Em quanto dura, e o favorece o vento.
Da herva, que renafce, fe apafcenta
O immenfo gado, que dos montes defce;

E

E renovando incendios deſta ſorte
A Arte emenda a Natureza, e podem
Ter ſempre nedio o gado, e o campo verde.
Mas agora ſabendo por eſpias
As noſſas marchas, conſervaváo ſempre
Secas as torradiſſimas campinas,
Nem conſentião, por fazer-nos guerra,
Que a chamma bemfeitora, e a cinza fria
Fertilizaſſe o arido terreno.
O cavallo até li forte, e brioſo,
E coſtumado a não ter mais ſuſtento,
Naquelles climas, do que a verde relva
Da mimoſa campina, desfalece.
Nem mais, ſe o ſeu Senhor o affaga, encurva
Os pés, e cava o chão co' as mãos, e o valle
Rinxando atroa, e açouta o ar co' as clinas.
Era alta noite, e carrancudo, e triſte
Negava o Ceo envolto em pobre manto

A

A luz ao Mundo, e murmurar fe ouvia

Ao longe o rio, e menear-fe o vento.

Refpirava defcanço a natureza.

Só na outra margem não podia em tanto

O inquieto Cacambo achar focego.

No perturbado interrompido fono,

Talvez foffe illusão, fe lhe aprefenta

A trifte imagem de Cepé defpido,

Pintado o rofto do temor da morte,

Banhado em negro fangue, que corria

Do peito aberto, e nos pizados braços

Inda os finaes da mifera cahida.

Sem adorno a cabeça, e aos pés calcada

A rota aljava, e as defcompoftas penas.

Quanto diverfo do Cepé valente,

Que no meio dos noffos efpalhava,

De pó, de fangue, e de fuor cuberto,

O efpanto, a morte! E diz-lhe em triftes vozes:
Fo-

Foge, foge, Cacambo. E tu deſcanças,
Tendo tão perto os inimigos? Torna,
Torna aos teus boſques, e nas patrias grutas
Tua fraqueza, e deſventura encobre.
Ou ſe acaſo inda vivem no teu peito
Os deſejos de gloria, ao duro paſſo
Reſiſte valeroſo; ah tu, que podes!
E tu, que podes, pőe a mão nos peitos
Á fortuna de Europa: agora he tempo,
Que deſcuidados da outra parte dormem.
Envolve em fogo, e fumo o campo, e paguem
O teu ſangue, e o meu ſangue. Aſſim dizendo
Se perdeo entre as nuvens, ſacudindo
Sobre as tendas no ar fumante toxa;
E aſſinala com chammas o caminho.
Acorda o Indio valeroſo, e ſalta
Longe da curva rede, e ſem demora
O arco, e as ſettas arrebata, e fere

O

O chão com o pé: quer fobre o largo rio

Ir peito a peito a contraftar co'a morte.

Tem diante dos olhos a figura

Do caro amigo, e inda lhe efcuta as vozes.

Pendura a hum verde tronco as varias penas,

E o arco, e as fettas, e a fonora aljava;

E onde mais manfo, e mais quieto o rio

Se eftende, e efpraia fobre a ruiva arêa,

Penfativo, e turbado entra; e com agua

Já por fima do peito as mãos, e os olhos

Levanta ao Ceo, que elle não via, e ás ondas

O corpo entrega. Já fabia em tanto

A nova empreza na limofa gruta

O patrio Rio; e dando hum geito á urna,

Fez que as aguas correffem mais ferenas;

E o Indio affortunado a praia oppofta

Tocou fem fer fentido. Aqui fe aparta

Da margem guarnecida, e manfamente

Pe-

Pelo filencio vai da noite efcura

Bufcando a parte, donde vinha o vento.

Lá, como he ufo do paiz, roçando

Dous lenhos entre fi, defperta a chamma,

Que já fe atea nas ligeiras palhas,

E velozmente fe propaga. Ao vento

Deixa Cacambo o refto, e foge a tempo

Da perigofa luz; porém na margem

Do rio, quando a chamma abrazadora

Começa a alumear a noite efcura,

Já fentido dos Guardas não fe affufta,

E temeraria, e venturofamente,

Fiando a vida aos animofos braços,

De hum alto precipicio ás negras ondas

Outra vez fe lançou, e foi de hum falto

Ao fundo rio a vifitar a arêa.

De balde gritão, e de balde ás margens

Corre a gente apreffada. Elle entre tanto

Sa-

Sacode as pernas, e os nervosos braços:
Rompe as escumas assoprando, e a hum tempo
Suspendido nas mãos, voltando o rosto,
Via nas aguas tremulas a imagem
Do arrebatado incendio, e se alegrava:
Não de outra sorte o cauteloso Ulisses,
Vaidoso da ruina, que causára,
Vio abrazar de Troia os altos muros,
E a perjura Cidade envolta em fumo
Encostar-se no chão, e pouco a pouco
Desmaiar sobre as cinzas. Cresce em tanto
O incendio furioso, e o irado vento
Arrebata ás mãos cheias vivas chammas,
Que aqui, e alli pela campina espalha.
Communica-se a hum tempo ao largo campo
A chamma abrazadora, e em breve espaço
Cérca as barracas da confusa gente.
Armado o General, como se achava,

                                          Sa-

Sahio do pavilhão, e prompto atalha,
Que não profiga o voador incendio.
Poucas tendas entrega ao fogo, e manda,
Sem mais demora, abrir largo caminho,
Que os fepare das chammas. Huns já cortão
As combuftiveis palhas, outros trazem
Nos promptos vafos as vizinhas ondas.
Mais não efpera o Barbaro atrevido.
A todos fe adianta; e defejofo
De levar a noticia ao grande Balda,
Naquella mefma noite o paffo eftende.
Tanto fe apreffa, que na quarta aurora
Por veredas occultas vjo de longe
A doce Patria, e os conhecidos montes,
E o Templo, que tocava o Ceo co' as grimpas.
Mas não fabia que a fortuna em tanto
Lhe preparava a ultima ruina.
Quanto feria mais ditofo! Quanto

Me-

Melhor lhe fora o acabar a vida
Na frente do inimigo, em campo aberto,
Ou fobre os reftos de abrazadas tendas,
Obra do feu valor! Tinha Cacambo
Real efpofa a fenhoril Lindoya,
De coftumes fuaviffimos, e honeftos
Em verdes annos: com ditofos laços
Amor os tinha unido; mas apenas
Os tinha unido, quando ao fom primeiro
Das trombetas lho arrebatou dos braços
A gloria enganadora. Ou foi que Balda
Engenhofo, e fubtil quiz desfazer-fe
Da prefença importuna, e perigofa
Do Indio generofo; e defde aquella
Saudofa manhã, que a defpedida
Prefenciou dos dous amantes, nunca
Confentio que outra vez tornaffe aos braços
Da formofa Lindoya, e defcubria

Sem-

Sempre novos pretextos da demora.

Tornar não esperado, e victorioso

Foi todo o seu delicto. Não consente

O cauteloso Balda que Lindoya

Chegue a fallar ao seu esposo; e manda

Que huma escura prizão o esconda, e aparte

Da luz do Sol. Nem os reaes parentes,

Nem dos amigos a piedade, e o pranto

Da enternecida esposa abranda o peito

Do obstinado Juiz: até que á força

De desgostos, de mágoa, e de saudade,

Por meio de hum licor desconhecido,

Que lhe deo compassivo o santo Padre,

Jaz o illustre Cacambo: entre os Gentios
Uni-

Por meio. Quanto a miudo os Jesuitas se sirvão de semelhante expediente nos casos mais apertados, só o póde ignorar quem nunca leo a Historia. A morte improvisa de Innocencio XIII, quando estava de todo resoluto a pôr cobro nas desordens dos Jesuitas, ainda não houve quem puzesse em dúvida ser obra dos mesmos. A mesma sorte teve o Cardeal Archin-

Unico, que na paz, e em dura guerra

De virtude, e valor deo claro exemplo.

Chorado occultamente, e fem as honras

De regio funeral, defconhecida

Pouca terra os honrados offos cobre.

Se he que os feus offos cobre alguma terra.

Crueis Miniftros, encubri ao menos

A funefta noticia. Ai que já fabe

A affuftada amantiffima Lindoya

O fucceffo infeliz. Quem a foccorre!

Que aborrecida de viver procura

Todos os meios de encontrar a morte.

Nem quer que o Efpofo longamente a efpere

No reino efcuro, aonde fe não ama.

        Mas

to. Em Roma he coufa pública, que o Cardeal Paf-
fionei morreo de hum *accidente Jefuitico.* Efte incom-
paravel Purpurado differa algumas vezes, que efpe-
raya ter o gofto de ver, antes da fua morte, a to-
tal extinção da Companhia. Os Jefuitas tiverão o
orgulho de fazer-lhe efte Epitafio: *Dominico S. R. E.*
Card. Paffion. S. J. fuperftes.

Mas a enrugada Tanajura, que era

Prudente, e exprimentada, e que a feus peitos

Tinha creado em mais ditofa idade

A mái da mái da mifera Lindoya,

E lia pela hiftoria do futuro,

Vizionaria, fuperfticiofa,

Que de abertos fepulcros recolhia

Nuas caveiras, e esburgados offos,

A huma medonha gruta, onde ardem fempre

Verdes candeias, conduzio chorando

Lindoya, a quem amava como filha;

E em ferrujento vafo licor puro

De viva fonte recolheo. Tres vezes

E   Gy-

Vizionaria. Os Indios davão-fe inteiramente á fu-
perftiçóes, e tinhão não fó por verofimil, fenão por
certa quanta extravagancia fe póde imaginar nefta
materia: vivião na mais craffa ignorancia. Não lhes
era licito faber mais do que aquillo, que podia fer-
vir de utilidade á Companhia. Toda a doutrina, que
lhes enfinavão, fe reduzia a atemorizallos com o In-
ferno, fe não obedeceffem em tudo, e por tudo aos
feus *fantos Padres.*

Gyrou em roda, e murmurou tres vezes

Co' a carcomida boca impias palavras,

E as aguas assoprou: depois com o dedo

Lhe impõe silencio, e faz que as aguas note.

Como no mar azul, quando recolhe

A lisonjeira viração as azas,

Adormecem as ondas, e retratão

Ao natural as debruçadas penhas,

O copado arvoredo, e as nuvens altas:

Não de outra sorte á timida Lindoya

Aquellas aguas fielmente pintão

O rio, a praia, o valle, e os montes, onde

Tinha sido Lisboa; e vio Lisboa

En-

Tinha sido Lisboa. He notorio quanto os Jesuitas abusárão, e pertendérão servir-se da calamidade pública para consternar os póvos, e reduzillos aos seus perniciosissimos interesses. De sorte, que a não ser a serenidade de animo do nosso amabilissimo Monarca, verdadeiramente imperturbavel, e a constancia do seu illuminadissimo Ministerio, ficava para sempre Portugal sepultado nas ruinas de Lisboa.

Entre defpedaçados edificios,
Com o folto cabello defcompofto,
Tropeçando em ruinas encoftar-fe.
Defamparada dos habitadores
A Rainha do Téjo, e folitaria,
No meio de fepulcros procurava
Com feus olhos foccorro; e com feus olhos
Só defcubria de hum, e de outro lado
Pendentes muros, e inclinadas torres.
Vê mais o Lufo Athlante, que forceja
Por fuftentar o pezo defmedido
Nos roxos hombros. Mas do Ceo fereno,
Em branca nuvem Provida Donzella
Rapidamente defce, e lhe aprefenta
De fua mão, Efpirito Conftante,
Genio de Alcides, que de negros monftros
Defpeja o Mundo, e enxuga o pranto á patria.
Tem por defpojos cabelludas pelles

E ij   De

De enfanguentadós, e famintos lobos,

E fingidas raposas. Manda, e logo

O incendio lhe obedece; e de repente

Por onde quer que elle encaminha os paffos,

Dáo lugar as ruinas. Vio Lindoya

Do meio dellas, fó a hum feu aceno,

Sahir da terra feitos, e acabados

Viftofos edificios. Já mais bella

Nafce Lisboa de entre as cinzas: gloria

Do grande Conde, que co' a máo robufta

Lhe firmou na alta tefta os vacillantes

Mal feguros caftellos. Mais ao longe

Promptas no Téjo, e ao curvo ferro atadas

Aos

Manda. Providencias fobre o Terremoto.

Dáo lugar. Defentulho da Cidade.

Sahir da terra. Reedificação de Lisboa dévida in-
teiramente á grandeza de coração de S. Mageftade,
e ao incanfavel efpirito do Illuftriffimo, e Excellen-
tiffimo Senhor Conde de Oeyras.

Promptas no Téjo. A Marinha Real no florentiffi-
mo eftado, em que a vemos, náo he a ultima glo-
ria defte feliciffimo Reinado; gloria, que fe deve

Aos olhos dão de fi terrivel moſtra,

Ameaçando o mar, as poderoſas

Soberbas náos. Por entre as cordas negras

Alvejão as bandeiras : geme atado

Na popa o vento; e·alegres, e viſtoſas

Deſcem das nuvens a beijar os mares

As ßamulas guerreiras. No horizonte

Já ſobre o mar azul apparecia

A pintada Serpente; obra, e trabalho

Do novo Mundo : que de longe vinha

Buſcar as nadadoras companheiras;

E já de longe a freſca Cintra, e os montes,

Que inda não conhecia, ſaudava.

Im-

principalmente ao zelo do Illuſtriſſimo, e Excellen-
tiſſimo Senhor Franciſco Xavier de Mendonça Fur-
tado.

    Serpente.·Náo feita no Rio de Janeiro, governan-
do o Illuſtriſſimo, e Excellentiſſimo Senhor Conde
de Cunha, embutida de peregrinas madeiras de di-
verſas cores, obra muito rara, e admiravel no ſeu
genero.

Impacientes da fatal demora
Os lenhos mercenarios junto á terra
Recebem no feu feio, e a outros climas,
Longe dos doces ares de Lisboa,
Tranfportão a Ignorancia, e a magra Inveja,
E envolta em negros, e compridos pannos
A Difcordia, o Furor. A torpe, e velha
Hypocrifia vagarofamente
Atrás delles caminha; e inda duvída
Que houveffe máo, que fe atreveffe a tanto.
O povo a moftra com o dedo; e ella
Com os olhos no chão da luz do dia
Foge, e cubrir o rofto inda procura
Com os pedaços do rafgado manto.
Vai, filha da ambição, onde te levão

O

Tranfportão. Só a pofteridade poderá juftamente
avaliar efta acção, que ferá fempre a mais brilhante
entre todas as do noffo tão applaudido Minifterio.
Sem fe fazer efte paffo, já mais poderia o Reino fa-
hir da ignorancia, em que o tinhão.

O vento, e os mares : pofsão teus alumnos

Andar errando fobre as aguas : poffa

Negar-lhe a bella Europa abrigo, e porto.

Alegre deixarei a luz do dia,

Se chegarem a ver meus olhos, que Adria

Da alta injuria fe lembra, e do feu feio

Te lança : e que te lanção do feu feio

Gallia, Iberia, e o paiz bello, que parte

O Apenino, e cinge o mar, e os Alpes.

Pareceo a Lindoya, que a partida

Deftes monftros deixava mais ferenos,

E

Que Adria. Por aquelle famofo interdicto de Paulo V os Jefuitas, que em humas efcabrofas circumftancias querião ter da fua parte a Curia, fahirão de Veneza, onde finalmente depois de meio Seculo tornárão a entrar. Parece incrivel que os Senhores Venezianos fe tenhão efquecido totalmente defta acção.

Gallia, Iberia. Quando o Author efcreveo eftes verfos eftava bem longe de imaginar que a maior parte do que nelles fe contém fe havia de cumprir em feus dias. Temos agora de mais a mais boas efperanças de ver cumprido brevemente o refto.

E mais puros os ares. Já se moſtra

Mais diſtincta a ſeus olhos a Cidade.

Mas vio, ai viſta laſtimoſa! a hum lado

Ir a fidelidade Portugueza

Manchados os puriſſimos veſtidos

De 'roxas nodoas. Mais ao longe eſtava

Com os olhos vendados, e eſcondido

Nas roupas hum punhal banhado em ſangue,

O Fanatiſmo, pela mão guiando

Hum curvo, e branco velho ao fogo, e ao laço.

Geme offendida a Natureza; e geme

Ai! muito tarde, a credula Cidade.

Os olhos póe no chão a Igreja irada,

E deſconhece, e deſapprova, e vinga

O

Hum curvo. Gabriel de Malagrida, diabolico mar-
tyr, que cá deixou a Companhia para ultima prova
do ſeu ſedicioſo, e fanatico eſpirito. Os Jeſuitas eſ-
palhárão pelos ſeus devotos em Roma huma eſtam-
pa com eſta letra: V. P. Gabr. Malagr. in Portugall.
pro fide occiſus.
    A Igreja. Foi relaxado ao braço ſecular, &c.

O delicto cruel, e a mão baſtarda.
Embebida na magica pintura
Goza as imagens vans, e não ſe atreve
Lindoya a perguntar. Vê deſtruida
A Republica infame, e bem vingada
A morte de Cacambo; e attenta, e immovel
Apaſcentava os olhos, e o deſejo,
E nem tudo entendia; quando a velha
Bateo co'a mão, e fez tremer as aguas.
Deſapparecem as fingidas torres,
E os verdes campos; nem já delles reſta
Leve final. Debalde os olhos buſcão
As náos: já não são náos; nem mar, nem
     montes,
Nem o lugar, onde eſtiverão. Torna
Ao pranto a faudoſiſſima Lindoya,
E de novo outra vez ſuſpira, e geme.
Até que a Noite compaſſiva, e attenta,
                    Que

Que as magoadas laſtimas lhe ouvíra,
Ao partir ſacudio das fuſcas azas,
Envolto em frio orvalho, hum leve ſomno,
Suave eſquecimento de ſeus males.

FIM DO CANTO TERCEIRO.

CANTO QUARTO

Salvas as Tropas do nocturno incendio,
Aos póvos se avizinha o grande Andrade,
Depois de assugentar os Indios fortes,
Que a subida dos montes defendião,
E rotos muitas vezes, e espalhados
Os Tapes cavalleiros, que arremeção
Duas causas de morte em huma lança,
E em largo gyro todo o campo escrevem.

Que

Que negue agora a perfida calumnia,

Que se ensinava aos barbaros gentios

A disciplina militar, e negue:

Que mãos traidoras a distantes póvos

Por asperos desertos conduzião

O pó sulfureo, e as sibilantes balas,

E o bronze, que rugia nos seus muros.

Tu que viste, e pizaste, ó Blasco insigne,

Todo aquelle paiz, tu só pudeste,

Co'a mão, que dirigia o ataque horrendo,

E

Que negue. Os Jesuitas, que hoje negão altamente a verdade de factos tão evidentes, fazião em outro tempo ostentacão disto mesmo. Os versos seguintes são do já citado Jesuita *Vanier* na digressão a respeito dos Indios do Paraguay. *Praed. rust. Lib. xiv.*

- - - - - - *arma, ducesque paratos*
Semper habent, Martisque truces formantur in usus.
Haec operum requies, sacris jam ritè peractis,
Timpanaque, & lituos festis audire diebus,
Et peditum turmas, equitumque videre sub armis.

Blasco. O Marechal D. Michel Angelo de Blasco Engenheiro mór do Reino.

E aplanava os caminhos á victoria,
Defcrever ao teu Rei o fitio, e as armas,
E os odios, e o furor, e a incrivel guerra.
Pizárão finalmente os altos rifcos
De efcalvada montanha, que os infernos
C' o pezo opprime, e a tefta altiva efconde
Na região, que não perturba o vento.
Qual vê quem foge á terra pouco á pouco
Ir crefcendo o Orizonte, que fe encurva,
Até que com os Ceos o mar confina,
Nem tem á vifta mais que o ar, e as ondas:
Affim quem olha do efcarpado cume
Não vê mais do que o Ceo, que o mais lhe
    encobre
A tarda, e fria nevoa, efcura, e denfa.
Mas quando o Sol de lá do eterno, e fixo
Purpureo encofto do dourado affento,
Co' a creadora mão desfaz, e corre

O

O véo cinzento de ondeadas nuvens,
Que alegre scena para os olhos! Podem
Daquella altura, por espaço immenso,
Ver as longas campinas retalhadas
De tremulos ribeiros; claras fontes,
E lagos cryftallinos, onde molha
As leves azas o lascivo vento.
Engraçados outeiros, fundos valles,
E arvoredos copados, e confusos,
Verde theatro, onde se admira quanto
Produzio a superflua Natureza.
A terra soffredora de cultura
Moftra o rasgado seio; e as varias plantas
Dando as mãos entre si, tecem compridas
Ruas, por onde a vifta saudosa
Se eftende, e perde. O vagaroso gado
Mal se move no campo, e se divísão
Por entre as sombras da verdura, ao longe,

                                        As

As cafas branquejando, e os altos Templos.

Ajuntaváo-fe os Indios entre tanto

No lugar mais vizinho, onde o bom Padre

Queria dar Lindoya por efpofa

Ao feu Baldetta, e fegurar-lhe o pofto,

E a Regia authoridade de Cacambo.

Eftáo patentes as douradas portas

Do grande Templo, e na vizinha Praça

Se váo difpondo de huma, e de outra banda

As viftofas efquadras differentes.

Co' a chata frente de Urucú tingida,

Vinha o Indio Kobbé disforme, e feio,

Que fuftenta nas mãos pezada maça,

Com que abate no campo os inimigos,

Como abate a feara o rijo vento.

Traz comfigo os falvages da montanha,

Que

O bom Padre. Balda.
Urucú. Rheed. Ericú mal. 2. p. 53. t. 31. Ve-ja-fe Linac. *Species plantarum.* Pentandr. Monog.

Que comem os feus mortos; nem confentem
Que já mais lhes efconda a dura terra
No feu avaro feio o frio corpo
Do doce pai, ou fufpirado amigo.
Foi o fegundo, que de fi fez moftra,
O mancebo Pindó, que fuccedêra.
A Cepé no lugar: inda em memoria
Do não vingado irmão, que tanto amava,
Leva negros penachos na cabeça.
São vermelhas as outras penas todas,
Côr, que Cepé ufára fempre em guerra.
Vão com elle os feus Tapes, que fe affrontão,
E que tem por injuria morrer velhos.
Segue-fe Caitutú de Regio fangue,
E de Lindoya irmão. Não muito fortes
São os que elle conduz; mas são tão deftros
No exercicio da frexa, que arrebatão
Ao verde papagaio o curvo bico,

Vo-

Voando pelo ar. Nem dos feus tiros

O peixe prateado eftá feguro

No fundo do ribeiro. Vinhão logo

Alegres Guaranís de amavel géfto.

Efta foi de Cacambo a efquadra antiga.

Penas da côr do Ceo trazem veftidas,

Com cintas amarelas: e Baldetta

Defvanecido a bella efquadra ordena

No feu Jardim: até o meio a lança

Pintada de vermelho, e a tefta, e o corpo

Todo cuberto de amarelas plumas.

Pendente a rica efpada de Cacambo;

E pelos peitos ao través lançada

Por fima do hombro efquerdo a verde faxa,

De donde ao lado oppofto a aljava defce.

N'um cavallo da côr da noite efcura

Entrou na grande Praça derradeiro

Tatú Guaçú feroz, e vem guiando

F Tro-

Tropel confuſo de cavalleria,

Que combate deſordenadamente.

Trazem lanças nas mãos, e lhes defendem

Pelles de monſtros os ſeguros peitos.

Revia-ſe em Baldetta o ſanto Padre;

E fazendo profunda reverencia,

Fóra da grande porta, recebia

O eſperado Tedêo aĉtivo, e prompto,

A quem acompanhava vagoroſo

Com as chaves no cinto o Irmão Patuſca,

De pezada, enormiſſima barriga.

Já mais a eſte o ſom da dura guerra

Tinha tirado as horas do deſcanço.

De indulgente moral, e brando peito,

Que penetrado da fraqueza humana

Soffre em paz as delicias deſta vida,

Taes,

A quem acompanhava. Eſte retrato he tirado ao natural de hum Leigo da Companhia, que o Author conhecco.

Taes, e quaes no-las dão. Gofta das coufas,
Porque gofta, e contenta-fe do effeito,
E nem fabe, nem quer faber as caufas.
Ainda que talvez, em falta de outro,
Com grofleiras acções o povo exhorte,
Gritando fempre, e fempre repetindo,
Que do bom Pai Adão a trifte raça
Por degráos degenera, e que efte Mundo
Peiorando envelhece. Não faltava,
Para fe dar principio á eftranha fefta,
Mais que Lindoya. Ha muito lhe preparão
Todas de brancas penas reveftidas
Feftóes de flores as gentís donzellas.
Canfados de efperar, ao feu retiro
Vão muitos impacientes a bufcalla.
Eftes de crefpa Tanajura aprendem
Que entrára no jardim trifte, e chorofa,
Sem confentir que alguem a acompanhaffe.

Hum frio fufto corre pelas veias

De Caitutú, que dèixa os feus no campo;

E a irmã por entre as fombras do arvoredo

Bufca co'a vifta, e teme de encontralla.

Entrão em fim na mais remota, e interna

Parte de antigo bofque, efcuro, e negro,

Onde ao pé de huma lapa cavernofa

Cobre huma rouca fonte, que murmura,

Curva latada de jafmins, e rofas.

Efte lugar deliciofo, e trifte,

Canfada de viver, tinha efcolhido

Para morrer a mifera Lindoya.

Lá reclinada, como que dormia,

Na branda relva, e nas mimofas flores,

Tinha a face na mão, e a mão no tronco

De

No jardim. Os Indios vivião na maior miferia, e apenas tinhão as coufas neceffarias abfolutamente para a vida. Os Padres porém vivião todos na abundancia, e tinhão jardins deliciofos, onde recolhião os efpiritos canfados de trabalhar na vinha do Senhor.

De hum funebre cipreſte, que eſpalhava
Melancolica ſombra. Mais de perto
Deſcobrem que ſe enrola no ſeu corpo
Verde ſerpente, e lhe paſſeia, e cinge
Peſcoço, e braços, e lhe lambe o ſeio.
Fogem de a ver aſſim ſobreſaltados,
E parão cheios de temor ao longe;
E nem ſe atrevem a chamalla, e temem
Que deſperte aſſuſtada, e irrite o monſtro,
E fuja, e apreſſe no fugir a morte.
Porém o deſtro Caitutú, que treme
Do perigo da irmã, ſem mais demora
Dobrou as pontas do arco, e quiz tres vezes
Soltar o tiro, e vacillou tres vezes
Entre a ira, e o temor. Em fim ſacode
O arco, e faz voar a aguda ſetta,
Que toca o peito de Lindoya, e 'fere
A ſerpente na teſta, e a boca, e os dentes
                                    Dei-

Deixou cravados no vizinho tronco.

Açouta o campo co'a ligeira cauda

O irado monſtro, e em tortuoſos gyros

Se enroſca no cipreſte, e verte envolto

Em negro ſangue o livido veneno.

Leva nos braços a infeliz Lindoya

O deſgraçado irmão, que aq deſpertalla

Conhece, com que dor! no frio roſto

Os ſinaes do veneno, e vè ferido

Pelo dente ſubtil o brando peito.

Os olhos, em que Amor reinava, hum dia,

Cheios de morte; e muda aquella lingua,

Que ao ſurdo vento, e aos échos tantas vezes

Contou a larga hiſtoria de ſeus males.

Nos olhos Caitutú não ſoffre o pranto,

E rompe em profundiſſimos ſuſpiros,

Lendo na teſta da fronteira gruta

De ſua mão já tremula gravado

O

O alheio crime, e a voluntaria morte.

E por todas as partes repetido

O suspirado nome de Cacambo.

Inda conserva o palido semblante

Hum não sei que de magoado, e triste,

Que os corações mais dur enternece.

Tanto era bella no seu rosto a mórte!

Indifferente admira o caso acerbo

Da estranha novidade alli trazido

O duro Balda; e os Indios, que se achavão,

Corre co'a vista, e os animos observa.

Quanto póde o temor! Seccou-se a hum tempo

Em mais de hum rosto o pranto; e em mais

de hum peito

Morrêrão suffocados os suspiros.

Ficou desamparada na espessura,

E exposta ás feras, e ás famintas aves,

Sem que alguem se atrevesse a honrar seu corpo

De

De poucas flores, e piedofa terra.

Faftofa Egypcia, que o maior triunfo

Temefte honrar do vencedor Latino,

Se defcefte inda livre ao efcuro reino,

Foi vaidofa talvez da imaginada

Barbara pompa do real fepulcro.

Amavel Indiana, eu te prometto

Que em breve a iniqua Patria envolta em
chammas

Te firva de urna, e que mifture, e leve

A tua, e a fua cinza o irado vento.

Confufamente murmurava em tanto

Do cafo atroz a laftimada gente.

Dizem que Tanajura lhe pintára

Suave aquelle genero de morte,

E talveź lhe moftraffe o fitio, e os meios.

Balda, que ha muito efpera o tempo, e o modo

De

Faftofa Egypcia. Cleopatra.

De alta vingança, e encobre a dor no peito,
Excita os póvos a exemplar caſtigo
Na deſgraçada velha. Alegre em roda
Se ajunta a petulante mocidade
Co' as armas, que o acaſo lhe offerece.
Mas neſte tempo hum Indio pelas ruas
Com géſto eſpavorido vem gritando,
Soltos, e arripiados os cabellos:
Fugí, fugí da mal ſegura terra,
Que eſtão já ſobre nós os inimigos.
Eu meſmo os vi, que deſcem do alto monte,
E vem cubrindo os campos; e ſe ainda
Vivo chego a trazer-vos a noticia,
Aos meus ligeiros pés a vida eu devo.
Debalde 'nos expomos neſte ſitio,
Diz o activo Tedêo: melhor conſelho
He ajuntar as Tropas no outro povo:
Perca-ſe o mais, ſalvemos a cabeça.
                                    Em-

Embora ſeja aſſim: faça-ſe em tudo
A vontade do Ceo; mas entre tanto
Vejão os contumazes inimigos
Que não tem que eſperar de nós deſpojos.
Falte-lhe a melhor parte ao ſeu triunfo.
Aſſim diſcorre Balda; e em tanto ordena,
Que todas as eſquadras ſe retirem,
Dando as caſas primeiro ao fogo, e o Templo.
Parte, deixando atada a triſte Velha
Dentro de huma choupana, e vingativo
Quiz que por ella começaſſe o incendio.
Ouvião-ſe de longe os altos gritos
Da miſeravel Tanajura. Aos ares
Vão globos eſpeſſiſſimos de fumo,
Que deixa enſanguentada a luz do dia.
Com as groſſas camaldulas á porta,
Devoto, e penitente os eſperava
O Irmão Patuſca, que ao rumor primeiro
　　　　　　　　　　　　　　　Ti-

Tinha fido o mais prompto a pôr-fe em falvo,

E a defertar da perigofa terra.

Por mais que o noffo General fe apreffe,

Não acha mais que as cinzas inda quentes,

E hum deferto, onde ha pouco era a Cidade.

Tinhão ardido as miferas choupanas

Dos pobres Indios, e no chão cahidos

Fumegavão os nobres edificios,

Deliciofa habitação dos Padres.

Entrão no grande Templo, e vem por terra

As imagens fagradas. O aureo throno,

O throno, em que fe adora hum Deos immen-

    menfo,

Que o foffre, e não caftiga os temerarios,

Em pedaços no chão. Voltava os olhos

                  Tur-

Entrão. Os noffos ainda confeguirão falvar o Templo, do qual fe remetteo a planta, e o profpecto a S. Mageftade. Os Padres tinhão mandado defpedaçar as Imagens, e reduzir a pequenas partes o Sacrario.

Turbado o General : aquella vista

Lhe encheo o peito de ira, e os olhos de
agua.

Em roda os seus fortissimos guerreiros

Admirão espalhados a grandeza

Do rico Templo, e os desmedidos arcos,

As bases das firmissimas columnas,

E os vultos animados, que respirão.

Na abobeda o artifice famoso

Pintára .... mas que intento! as roucas vo-
zes

Seguir não podem do pincel os rasgos.

Genio da inculta America, que inspiras

A meu peito o furor, que me transporta,

Tu me levanta nas seguras azas.

Se-

Admirão. O General não se podia persuadir, que
os riquissimos ornamentos tivessem sido bordados na-
quelle Paiz, até que se lhe mostrou hum, que foi
achado junto á Sacristia ainda imperfeito no tear.

Serás em paga ouvido no meu canto.
E te prometto, que pendente hum dia
Adorne a minha lyra os teus altares.

FIM DO CANTO QUARTO.

CAN-

CANTO QUINTO

NA vasta, e curva abobeda pintára
A destra máo de artifice famoso,
Em breve espaço, e Villas, e Cidades,
E Provincias, e Reinos. No alto solio

Es-

Na vasta. As façanhas dos Jesuitas não estavão sepultadas só no Uraguay. Quem se admirar da pintura deste Templo, considere attentamente a que elles tem na Igreja do seu Collegio Romano, e na da Casa Professa, que com estar cubertas da mascara da Religião, não deixão de ser ainda mais soberbas, e insultantes.

Eſtava dando leis ao Mundo inteiro

A Companhia. Os Sceptros, e as Coroas,

E as Tyaras, e as Purpuras em torno

Semeadas no cháo. Tinha de hum lado

Dadivas corruptoras: do outro lado

Sobre os brancos altares ſuſpendidos

Agudos ferros, que gotejáo ſangue.

Por eſta máo ao pé dos altos muros

Hum dos Henriques perde a vida, e o Reino.

E cahe por eſta máo, oh Ceos! debalde

Rodeado dos ſeus o outro Henrique.

                          De-

Hum dos Henriques. Henrique III aſſaſſinado por Fr. Jacques Clemente. Quem ha que ignore quanta parte tiverão niſto os Jeſuitas ? He público o proceſſo do P. Guignard, e quanto a Companhia defende ainda hoje eſte ſeu digno filho. Vejão-ſe os ſeus Authores, e por todos o Jovency.

O outro Henrique. Na morte de Henrique IV ſoube-ſe eſconder melhor a mao Jeſuitica ; mas não ſe ſoube eſconder nas duas occaſiões antecedentes, em que ſe tinha intentado o meſmo parricidio. O Padre Varade, Superior da Companhia em Paris, foi quem

Delicia do feu povo, e dos humanos.

Principes, o feu fangue he voffa offenfa.

Novos crimes prepara o horrendo monftro,

Armai o braço vingador : defcreva

Seus tortos fulcos o luzente arado

Sobre o feu throno; nem aos tardos netos

O lugar, em que foi, moftrar-fe poffa.

Viáo-fe ao longe errantes, e efpalhados

Pelo Mundo os feus filhos ir lançando

Os fundamentos do efperado Imperio,

De dous em dous : ou fobre os coroados

G   Mon-

defencaminhou ao miferavel Barriere : levou-o ao feu
cubiculo, deitou-lhe a fua bençáo, confeffou-o, deo-
lhe depois a communháo, &c. Os Jefuitas no Col-
legio de Clermont, e na fua Igreja de Santo Anto-
nio, por meio de práticas, conferencias, medita-
çóes, e exercicios efpirituaes corrompérão o efpirito
de Chatel.

Novos crimes. Tragáo-fe k memoria a tarde de 5
de Janeiro, e a noite de 3 de Setembro táo funef-
tas para França, e Portugal, e que podião cubrir
de luto eftas duas Monarquias.

Montes do Téjo; ou nas remotas praias,

Que habitão as pintadas Amazonas,

Por onde o Rei das aguas efcumando

Foge da eftreita terra, e infulta os mares.

Ou no Ganges fagrado; ou nas efcuras

Nunca de humanos pés trilhadas ferras,

Aonde o Nilo tem, fe he que tem fonte.

Com hum géfto innocente aos pés do throno

Via-fe a Liberdade Americana,

Que arraftando enormiffimas cadeias,

Sufpira, e os olhos, e a inclinada tefta

Nem

O feu throno. O throno da Companhia eftá em Roma. Lá he o centro do feu poder. Alli recebe o feu Geral os avifos do que fe paffa em todas as partes do Mundo : e dalli com o maior defpotifmo envia as fuas ordens ao fim da terra. Exterminalla das outras Provincias he fazer-lhe guerra pela rama : he neceffario cortar-lhe a raiz. Ora os thefouros das duas Indias ajudavão muito a fuftentar o credito dos Jefuitas em Roma. Affortunadamente as prefentes difpofições todas annuncião a proxima total extinção daquelle Corpo.

Nem levanta, de humilde, e de medrofa.

Tem diante riquiffimo tributo,

Brilhante pedraria, e prata, e ouro,

Funefto preço, por que compra os ferros.

Ao longe o mar azul, e as brancas vélas,

Com eftranhas divifas nas bandeiras,

Denotão que afpirava ao fenhorio,

E da navegação, e do commercio.

Outro tempo, outro clima, outros coftumes.

Mais além tão diverfa de fi mefma

G ii   Vef-

De dons em dons. Os Jefuitas em Portugal erão chamados os Apoftolos: e efcrupulofamente obfervavão a exterioridade do *mifit illos binos.*

Rei das aguas. O Rio das Amazonas por huma boca de oitenta leguas fahe encanado com tal força, que lança por muitas leguas ao mar agua doce.

Aonde o Nilo tem. Os Jefuitas até fe jactão nas fuas Hiftorias de tér defcuberto a origem do Nilo.

Nem levanta. Não ha palavras, que expliquem baftantemente a fujeição, em que vivião aquelles Indios. Vejão-fe os fragmentos das Cartas do Conde de Bobadela citadas na *Republica*, &c.

Veſtida em larga roupa fluctuante,

Que diſtinguem barbaricos lavores,

Reſpira no ar Chinez o mole faſto

De aſiatica pompa; e grave, e lenta

Permitte aos Bonzos, a pezar de Roma,

Do ſeu Legislador o indigno culto.

Aqui entrando no Japão fomenta

Domeſticas diſcordias. Lá paſſea

No meio dos eſtragos, oſtentando

Orvalhadas de ſangue as negras roupas.

Cá

As brancas vélas. Os Jeſuitas do Brazil tinhão hu-
ma fragata magnifica, em que o Provincial ſahia to-
dos os annos a titulo de viſitar a Provincia: porém
na realidade era a que fazia a maior parte do com-
mercio, que aquelles portos tem entre ſi. Em quan-
to a fragata recebia carga, eſtavão ocioſas todas as
outras embarcações: ſendo os fretes daquella mais
caros, a titulo de ir a fazenda mais ſegura. Ora os
Jeſuitas nas Alfandegas nunca pagárão direitos. O
ſeu lucro era immenſo. Para ſe conſeguir melhor eſte
fim, eſpalhárão pelo povo huma profecia do ſeu Pa-
dre Anchieta, que aquella fragata nunca ſe perde-

Cá deſterrada em fim dos ricos portos,

Voltando aviſta ás terras, que perdêra,

Quer pizar temeraria, e criminoſa ...

Oh Ceos! que negro horror! tinha ficado

Imperfeita a pintura, e envolta em ſombras.

Tremeo a máo do artifice ao fingilla,

E deſmaiárão no pincel as cores.

Da parte oppoſta, nas ſoberbas praias

Da rica Londres tragica, e funeſta,

Enſanguentado o Tamega eſmorece,

Vendo a conjuração perfida, e negra,

Que

ria. Encalharão-na finalmente, e fizerão outra, que
cuſtou ſincoenta mil cruzados. E ſendo-lhes neceſſa-
rio perpetuar aquella ſanta impoſtura, mandárão pre-
gar na nova algumas taboas da velha: e perſuadirão
áquelles bons negociantes, que baſtava aquella par-
te para communicar a virtude ao todo. O Author
vio muitas vezes eſta fragata, e entrou nella. Tra-
zia flamula, e bandeira com a inſignia da Compa-
nhia ; e tinha de mais a mais excellente artilheria.
Ao entrar, e ſahir dos portos recebia todas as hon-
ras, que ſe fazem ás náos do Rei.

Que fe prepara ao crime; e intenta, e efpera

Erguer aos Ceos nos inflammados hombros,

E efpalhar pelas nuvens denegridos

Todos os grandes, e a famofa falla.

Por entre os troncos de humas plantas negras,

Por obra fua, vião-fe arraftados

Ás ardentes arêas Africanas

O valor, e alta gloria Portugueza.

Ai mal aconfelhado, quanto forte,

Generofo Mancebo! eternos lutos

Preparas á chorofa Lufitania.

De-

Mais além. Os Jefuitas da China no anno de 1645 aprovcitárão-fe da divisão daquelle grande Imperio, entre os dous pertendentes, para o entregarem ao Kam dos Tartaros. Forão em premio elevados á dignidade de Mandarins, e ornados com os ricos veftidos, e colares, que fe podem ver na eftampa, que nos deixou o P. Bonani no *Catulogo dos Religiofos, &c.*

Permitte. E de mais a mais o fervirem-fe, para nomear o verdadeiro Deos, das vozes *Tien Cco*, e *Xanti* fupremo Emperador: e fazerem certas oblaçóes aos feus defuntos.

Defejado dos teus, a incertos climas

Vás mendigar a morte, e a fepultura.

Já fatisfeitos do fatal defignio,

Por máo de hum dos Filippes, affogaváo

Nos abyfmos do mar, e emudeciáo

Queixofas linguas, e fagradas bocas,

Em que ainda fe ouvia a voz da Patria.

Crefcia o feu poder, e fe firmava

Entre furdas vinganças. Ao mar largo

Lança do profanado occulto feio

O irado Téjo os frios nadadores.

E

Bonzos. Sacerdotes da China.

A pezar de Roma. E bem a pezar della, que em fim canfou de lutar por mais de hum feculo com a animozidade dos Jefuitas. O fruto, que fe tirou dos Decretos das Sagradas Congregaçóes publicados em 1645, foi o que tirou Monfig. Maigrot em 1693, o Cardeal de Tournon em 1704, Clemente XI em 1710, Benedicto XIII em 1727, Clemente XII em 1734, Benedicto XIV em 1742. Com tudo ifto ainda hoje não cefsão de repetir que são a guarda pretoriana do Papa; e o mais he que fallão verdade:

En fes

E deixa o barco, e foge para a praia

O pefcador, que attonito recolhe

Na longa rede o pálido cadaver

Privado de fepulcro. Em quanto os noffos

Apafcentáo a vifta na pintura,

Nova empreza, e outro genero de guerra

Em fi revolve o General famofo.

Apenas efperou que ao Sol brilhante

Déffe as coftas de todo a opaca terra;

Precipitou a marcha, e no outro povo

Foi forprender os Indios. O cruzeiro,

Con-

En fes Pretoriens Rome eut autant defraitres,
Ils marchandaient l' Empire, e lui donnaient des maitres.
　Le Philofophe de Sans-fouci dans l' Epitre a Darget.

Legislador. Confucio.

Que perdéra. *Qualia forte dolent dites Orientis ad oras*
　- - - - erepta - - - fibi regna. - - -
　　　　　Vanier. fupr.

Quer pizar. Os Jefuitas com as fuas reftriccóes
mentaes não duvidárão ao principio calcar o cruci-

Conftellação dos Europeos não vifta,

As horas declinando lhe affinala.

A córada manhã ferena, e pura

Começava a bordar nos horizontes

O Ceo de brancas nuvens povoado,

Quando, abertas as portas, fe defcobrem

Em trages de caminho ambos os Padres,

Que manfamente do lugar fugião,

Defamparando os miferaveis Indios,

Depois de expoftos ao furor das armas.

Lobo voraz, que vai na fombra efcura

Me-

fixo, por não perderem aquelle riquiffimo commer-
cio. Quem quizer fazer conceito da extensão defte,
e de outras curiofidades nefta materia, lea as via-
gens de Mr. Duquefne mandado por Luiz XIV ás
Indias Orientaes. Tom. 3. pag. 81.

A conjuração. Os Padres Garnet, e Oldecorne
réos convictos, e confeffos da conjuração da polvora.

Nos abyfmos do mar. Veja-fe a *Dedução Chronolo-
gica*: Obra, que fervirá de Epoca á reftauração das
Letras em Portugal ; monumento de zelo, e de fi-
delidade.

Meditando traições ao manso gado,
Perseguido dos cães, e descuberto
Não arde em tanta colera, como ardem
Balda, e Tedêo. A soldadesca alegre
Cérca em roda o fleugmatico Patusca,
Que próvido de longe os acompanha,
E mal se move no jumento tardo.
Pendem-lhe dos arções de hum lado, e de
      outro
Os paios saborosos, e os vermelhos
Presuntos Europeos; e a tiracolo
Inseparavel companheira antiga
De seus caminhos a borraxa pende.
Entra no povo, e ao Templo se encaminha
O invicto Andrade; e generoso em tanto
Reprime a militar licença, e a todos
Co' a grande sombra ampara: alegre, e brando
No meio da victoria. Em roda o cércão,
              (Nem

(Nem fe énganárão) procurando abrigo
Chorofas máis, e filhos innocentes,
E curvos pais, e timidas donzellas.
Socegado o tumulto, e conhecidas
As vís aftucias de Tedêo, e Balda,
Cahe a infame Republica por terra.
Aos pés do General as tofcas armas
Já tem depofto o rude Americano,
Que reconhece as ordens, e fe humilha,
E a imagem do feu Rei proftrado adora.

Serás lido Uraguay. Cubra os meus olhos
Embora hum dia a efcura noite eterna.
Tu vive, e goza a luz ferena, e pura.
Vai aos bofques de Arcadia: e não receies
Chegar defconhecido áquella arêa.
Alli de frefco entre as fombrias murtas
Urna trifte a Miréo não todo enferra.

Le-

Leva de eſtranho Ceo, ſobre ella eſpalha
Co' a peregrina mão barbaras flores.
E buſca o ſucceſſor, que te encaminhe
Ao teu lugar, que ha muito que te eſpera.

FIM DO CANTO QUINTO.

AO

AO AUTHOR

SONETO

PArece-me que vejo a grossa enchente,
E a villa errante, que nas aguas boya:
Detesto os crimes da infernal tramoya:
Choro a Cacambo, e a Cepé valente.

Não he pressagio vão: lerá a gente
A guerra do Uraguay, como a de Troya;
E o lagrimoso caso de Lindoya
Fará sentir o peito, que não sente.

Ao longe, a Inveja hum paiz ermo, e bronco
Infecte com seu halito perverso,
Que a ti só chega o mal distincto ronco.

Ah! consente que o meu junto ao teu verso,
Qual fraca vide, q̃ se arrima a hum tronco,
Tambem vá discorrer pelo Universo.

De Joaquim Ignacio de Seixas Brandão, Doutor em
Medicina pela Universidade de Montpellier.

AO

ao Author

SONETO

ENtro pelo Uraguay: vejo a cultura
Das novas terras por engenho claro;
Mas chego aò Templo mageſtoſo, e paro
Embebido nos raſgos da pintura.

Vejo erguer-ſe a Republica perjura
Sobre alicerces de hum dominio avaro:
Vejo diſtinctamente, ſe reparo,
De Caco uſurpador a cova eſcura.

Famoſo Alcides, ao teu braço forte
Toca vingar os ſceptros, e os altares:
Arranca a eſpada, deſcarrega o còrte.

E tu, Termindo, leva pelos ares
A grande acçaõ; já que te coube em ſorte
A glorioſa parte de a cantares.

Do Doutor Ignacio Joſé de Alvarenga Peixoto,
graduado na faculdade de Leis pela Univerſi-
dade de Coimbra.

SELECTED
BIBLIOGRAPHY

1. Editions of *O Uraguai* (all)

   O Uraguai. Poema de José Basílio da Gama. Na Arcádia de Roma Termindo Sipílio. Dedicado ao Ilmo. e Exmo. Senhor Francisco Xavier de Mendonça Furtado Secretário de Estado de S. Majestade Fidelíssima, etc. Lisbon: Régia Oficina Tipográfica, 1769.

   O Uraguai. Poema de José Basílio da Gama, na Arcádia de Roma Termindo Sipílio. Nova Edição. Rio de Janeiro: Imprensa Régia, 1811.

   O Uraguai, Poema de José Basílio da Gama, na Arcádia de Roma Termindo Sipílio. Nova Edição. Lisbon: Impressão de João Nunes Esteves, 1822.

   Minerva Brasiliense. Biblioteca Brasílica, ou Coleção de Obras Originais, ou Traduzidas de Autores Célebres. Tomo I. Uraguai, Poema de José Basílio de Gama. Na Arcádia de Roma Termindo Sipílio. Rio de Janeiro: Tipografia Austral, 1844. Edition probably known to Burton.

   Épicos Brasileiros. O Uraguai por José Basílio da Gama e O Caramuru por Fr. José de Santa Rita Durão. Lisbon: Imprensa Nacional, 1845. Edition prepared by Francisco Adolfo de Varnhagen, assisted by A. J. da Serra Gomes. Used by Burton.

   O Uraguai. Poema de José Basílio da Gama. Na Arcádia de Roma Termindo Sipílio. Rio de Janeiro: "Marmota Fluminense," Empresa Tipográfica Dous de Dezembro, 1855. The poem appeared in successive editions of the magazine *Marmota Fluminense,* nos. 559-568, 569-570 (9-30 March, 3-6 April 1855).

   O Uraguai. Poema de José Basílio da Gama. Na Arcádia de Roma Termindo Sipílio. Nova Edição. Rio de Janeiro: Empresa Tipográfica Dous de Dezembro, Paula Brito, 1855. Edition known to Burton.

   O Uraguai. Rio de Janeiro: Tipografia da Escola do Editor, Serafim José Alves, n.d.

252 SELECTED BIBLIOGRAPHY

Galeria de Escritores Brasileiros. José Basílio da Gama. O Uraguai. Precedido de um Estudo Crítico por Francisco Pacheco. Rio de Janeiro: Francisco Alves, 1895.
José Basílio da Gama. O Uraguai. Poema-Épico com Anotações de J. Artur Montenegro. Pelotas, Rio Grande do Sul: Echenique Irmãos, 1900.
Coleção de Autores Célebres da Literatura Brasileira. Obras Poéticas de José Basílio da Gama. Precedidas de uma Biografia Crítica e Estudo Literário do Poeta por José Veríssimo. Rio de Janeiro; Paris: Garnier, n.d. Published in 1902, this is the only edition of Basílio da Gama's complete works.
O Uraguai. Poema. Edição Publicações do Centenário em Minas Gerais. Coletânea de Autores Mineiros Organizada por Mário de Lima. Poetas. Vol. I. Escola Mineira. Pré-Românticos. Belo Horizonte: Imprensa Oficial, 1922.
José Basílio da Gama. O Uraguai. Edição Comemorativa do Segundo Centenário Anotada por Afrânio Peixoto, Rodolfo Garcia e Osvaldo Braga. Rio de Janeiro: Academia Brasileira de Letras, 1941. Facsimile of the 1769 edition.
———. *O Uraguai por Mário Camarinha da Silva* ed. Rio de Janeiro: AGIR, 1964.

2. Other works by José Basílio da Gama (all)

Epitalâmio da Exma. Sra. D. Mária Amália por José Basílio da Gama, na Arcádia de Roma Termindo Sipílio. Lisbon: Oficina de José da Silva Nazaré, 1769.
A Declamação Trágica: poema Dedicado às Belas-Artes. Lisbon: Régia Oficina Tipográfica, 1772. Paraphrase of one canto of Claude Joseph Dorat's *La Déclamation Théâtrale.*
A Liberdade, do Sr. Pedro Metastásio, Poeta Cesáreo, com a Tradução Francesa de Mr. Rousseau, de Genebra, e a Portuguesa de Termindo, Poeta Árcade. Lisbon: Régia Oficina Tipográfica, 1773.
Soneto ao Rei D. José no Dia da Inauguração da sua Estátua Eqüestre. Loose sheet, signed José Basílio da Gama, 6 June 1775.
Os Campos Elíseos, Oitavas de Termindo Sipílio, Pastor da Arcádia aos Ilmos. e Exmos. Condes da Redinha. Lisbon: Régia Oficina Tipográfica, 1776.
Soneto Extemporâneo à Aclamação de D. Maria I. Loose sheet signed "Termindo, Pastor da Arcádia, 1777."
Lenitivo da Saudade na Morte do Sermo. Sr. D. José, Príncipe do Brasil, por um Anônimo. Lisbon: Oficina de Lino da Silva Godinho, 1778.
Quitúbia. Lisbon: Oficina de Antônio Rodrigues Galhardo, 1791.

3. Works on José Basílio da Gama

Kaulen, Lorenz. *Reposta* [sic] *Apologética ao Poema Intitulado "O Uraguai," Composto por José Basílio da Gama e Dedicado a Francisco Xavier de Mendonça Furtado, Irmão de Sebastião José de Carvalho e Melo, Conde de Oeiras e Marquês de Pombal.* Lugano: n.p., 1786. Reprinted as "Refutação das Calúnias contra os Jesuítas Contidas no Poema 'Uraguai' de José Basílio da Gama." *Revista do Instituto Historico e Geográfico Brasileiro* 68 (1907):93-224.

Denis, Ferdinand. *Résumé de l'histoire littéraire du Portugal et du Brésil.* Paris: Lecoint et Durey, 1826. Pp. 554-566. Mentioned by Burton.

Barbosa, Januário da Cunha. *Parnaso Brasileiro, ou Coleção das Melhores Poesias dos Poetas do Brasil, tanto Inéditas como já Impressas.* 2 vols. Rio de Janeiro: Tipografia Imperial e Nacional, 1829-1831.

Garrett, João Batista da Silva Leitão de Almeida. *Bosquejo da Poesia Portuguesa.* 1826; rpt. in *Obras Completas,* Lisbon: Empresa da História de Portugal, 1904. 21:31. Mentioned by Burton.

Revista Trimensal do Instituto Histórico-Geográfico Brasileiro. 1 (1839):152-155. "A short and unsatisfactory sketch of Basílio da Gama's life." [Burton]

Silva, João Manuel Pereira da. *Plutarco Brasileiro.* 2 vols. Rio de Janeiro: Laemmert, 1847. Rpt. as *Os Varões Ilustres do Brasil durante os Tempos Coloniais.* 2 vols. Paris: A. Franck, 1858. Known to Burton, who might have also known a much improved edition printed by Laemmert in 1868.

Costa e Silva, José Maria da. *Ensaio Biográfico-Crítico sobre os Melhores Poetas Portugueses.* Lisbon: Imprensa Silviana, 1853. 4:208.

Silva, Inocêncio Francisco da. *Dicionário Bibliográfico Português. Estudos Aplicáveis a Portugal e ao Brasil.* 22 vols. Lisbon: Imprensa Nacional, 1858-1923. 4 (1860):268-270. Consulted by Burton.

Wolf, Ferdinand. *Le Brésil littéraire.* Berlin: Ascher, 1863. Mentioned by Burton. Pp. 50-60. Available in Portuguese as *O Brasil Literário,* trad. Jamil Almansur Haddad. São Paulo: Companhia Editora Nacional, 1959.

Major, Manuel Antônio. "*Uraguai,* Poema Épico de José Basílio da Gama," *Revista Mensal da Sociedade Ensaios Literários,* 2 (1864):419-426.

Reis, Francisco Sotero dos. *Curso de Literatura Portuguesa e Brasileira.* 5 vols. São Luís do Maranhão: Tipografia do País, 1862-1868. 4:201-230.

Assis, Joaquim Maria Machado de. "Literatura Brasileira: Instinto de Nacionalidade." *Crítica Literária.* Rio de Janeiro: Jackson, 1946. Originally printed in *O Novo Mundo,* Ano 3, New York, 1872.

Cabral, Alfredo do Vale. *Anais da Imprensa Nacional do Rio de Janeiro de 1808 a 1822.* Rio de Janeiro: Tipografia Nacional, 1881. Pp. 72-74.

Romero, Sílvio. *História da Literatura Brasileira.* 2 vols. 1888; rpt. 5 vols. Rio de Janeiro: José Olympio, 1943. 2:82-88.

Ferreira, Félix. *Basílio da Gama.* Rio de Janeiro: Jornal do Comércio, 1895.

Lima, Manuel de Oliveira. *Aspectos da Literatura Colonial Brasileira.* Leipzig: Brockhaus, 1896. Pp. 219-221.

Blake, Augusto Vitorino Alves Sacramento. *Dicionário Bibliográfico Brasileiro.* 7 vols. Rio de Janeiro: Imprensa Nacional, 1898. 4:331-332.

Braga, Teófilo. *Filinto Elísio e os Dissidentes da Arcádia.* Porto: Lelo, 1901. Pp. 480-505.

Veríssimo, José. *Estudos de Literatura Brasileira.* 6 vols. Rio de Janeiro: Garnier, 1901. 2:89-129.

———. *História da Literatura Brasileira.* Rio de Janeiro: Francisco Alves, 1916. Pp. 109-129. 3d ed. Rio de Janeiro: José Olympio, 1954.

Carvalho, Ronald de. *Pequena História da Literatura Brasileira.* 1919; rpt. Rio de Janeiro: Briguiet, 1935. Pp. 153-159.

Mota, Artur. *Vultos e Livros.* São Paulo: Monteiro Lobato, 1921. Pp. 69-80.

Guerra, Álvaro. *Basílio da Gama.* São Paulo: Melhoramentos, 1923.

Cavalcanti, Povina. *Telhado de Vidro.* Rio de Janeiro: A. Pernambucana, 1928. Pp. 115-154.

Pinto, Manuel de Sousa. *O Indianismo na Poesia Brasileira.* Coimbra: Coimbra Editora, 1928. Reprint from *Biblos* 4 (1928):35-56.

Mota, Artur. *História da Literatura Brasileira: Época de Formação (Séculos XVI e XVII).* 2 vols. São Paulo: Editora Nacional, 1930. 2:258-272.

Le Gentil, Georges. *La Littérature Portugaise.* Paris: Armand Colin, 1935. Pp. 122-123.

Franco, Afonso Arinos de Melo. *O Índio Brasileiro e a Revolução Francesa. As Origens Brasileiras da Teoria da Bondade Natural.* Rio de Janeiro: José Olympio, 1937. Pp. 261-263.

Paranhos, Haroldo. *História do Romantismo no Brasil.* São Paulo: Cultura Brasileira, 1937. Pp. 135-151.

Lélis, Carlindo. "Basílio da Gama e *O Uraguai.*" *Revista das Academias de Letras* 9, 26 (Oct. 1940):129-147.

Santos, Lúcio José dos. "A Companhia de Jesus." *Estudos Brasileiros.* 5, 13-14 (July-Oct. 1940):27-63.

Braga, Osvaldo. "*O Uraguai* e suas Edições: Nota Bibliográfica de O. B." *O Uraguai.* . . . Rio de Janeiro: Academia Brasileira de Letras, 1941. Pp. 153-277.

Calmon, Pedro. "Discurso na Sessão Pública do Segundo Centenário de Basílio da Gama." *Revista da Academia Brasileira de Letras* 62 (1941):211-226.

Carneiro, Levi. "Discurso." *Revista da Academia Brasileira de Letras* 62 (1941):206-209.

Leite, Padre Serafim. "Basílio da Gama Jesuíta." *Revista da Academia Brasileira de Letras* 62 (1941):209-211.

Sousa, Cláudio de. "José Basílio da Gama." *Revista da Academia Brasileira de Letras* 62 (1941):227-249.

Peixoto, Afrânio. "Nota Preliminar." *O Uraguai.* . . . Rio de Janeiro, 1941. Pp. vii-xxxvii.

Driver, David Miller. *The Indian in Brazilian Literature.* New York: Hispanic Institute in the United States, 1942. Pp. 24-27.

Lima, Henrique de Campos Ferreira. "José Basílio da Gama: Alguns Novos Subsídios para a sua Biografia." *Brasília* 2 (1943):15-32.

Nunes, Arnaldo. "Basílio da Gama." *Revista da Academia Fluminense de Letras* 1 (Oct. 1949):203-217.

Holanda, Sérgio Buarque de. "Uma Epopéia Americana." *Diário Carioca,* 27 Dec. 1953, p. 20.

Dutra, Waltensir. "Basílio da Gama." *A Literatura no Brasil.* 6 vols. Ed. Afrânio Coutinho. Rio de Janeiro: Sul Americana, 1955. 1:494-502.

Gomes, Eugênio. *Visões e Revisões.* Rio de Janeiro: INL, 1958. Pp. 38-45.

Oliveira, Martins de. *História da Literatura Mineira.* Belo Horizonte: Itatiaia, 1958. Pp. 60-65.

Amora, Antônio Soares et al. *Panorama da Poesia Brasileira,* vol. 1. *Era Luso-Brasileira.* Rio de Janeiro: Civilização Brasileira, 1959. Pp. 143-169.

Cândido (de Melo e Sousa), Antônio. *Formação da Literatura Brasileira.* 2 vols. São Paulo: Martins, 1959. 2d ed. 1964. 1:133-142.

―――. *Literatura e Sociedade: Estudos de Teoria e História Literária.* São Paulo: Editora Nacional, 1967. Pp. 118-119, 223-229.

Martins, Heitor. "O Senhor Cá-Qui." *Minas Gerais, Suplemento Literário,* 16 March 1968, p. 4.

Cândido (de Melo e Sousa), Antônio. "O Ritmo do Mundo." *Minas Gerais, Suplemento Literário,* 7 Sept. 1968, p. 8.

Cândido (de Melo e Sousa), Antônio. "A Dois Séculos d'*O Ura-guai*." *Vários Escritos*. São Paulo: Duas Cidades, 1970. Pp. 161-188.

Peres, Fernando da Rocha. "Um Inédito de Basílio da Gama." *Luso-Brazilian Review* 10, 2 (Winter 1973):241-246. Recent discovery of manuscript of Gama's sonnet attacking the Regedor Cardinal da Cunha.

Garcia, Frederick C. H. "*O Uraguai*: Alguns Problemas de uma Tradução Inédita." *Minas Gerais, Suplemento Literário*, 7 Sept. 1974, pp. 2-5. A firsthand treatment of Burton's translation.

————. "Richard Francis Burton and Basílio da Gama: The Translator and the Poet." *Luso-Brazilian Review* 13, 1 (Summer 1975):34-57. An extended version of the previous entry.

Hulet, Claude L. *Brazilian Literature*. 2 vols. Washington, D.C.: Georgetown University Press, 1974-1975. 1:90-100.

Martins, Wilson. *História da Inteligência Brasileira*. São Paulo: Cultrix, 1977. 1:422-439.

4.   Related works by Sir Richard F. Burton

"From London to Rio de Janeiro. Letters to a Friend." *Fraser's Magazine for Town and Country* 72 (1865):492-503; 73 (1866):78-92.

The Highlands of the Brazil. 2 vols. 1869; rpt. New York: Greenwood Press, 1969. Especially 1:143-145.

Letters from the Battle-fields of Paraguay. London: Tinsley Brothers, 1870. In the introductory essay, Burton gives a history of the Jesuits in the Paraguayan reductions (pp. 25-35). In letter 4 ("To the Colonia and Buenos Aires") he discusses the "endless question" of Colônia do Sacramento.

"Translation," *The Athenaeum*, no. 2313 (24 Feb. 1872), pp. 241-243.

The Lands of Cazembe. Lacerda's Journey to Cazembe in 1798. Translated and Annotated by Captain R. F. Burton. . . . London: Royal Geographical Society (John Murray), 1873. Burton apparently worked on this book during his stay in Brazil; it deals with the adventures of a Portuguese explorer in central Africa.

"Notes on the Kitchen-Middens of São Paulo, Brazil, and the Footprints of St. Thomas, Alias Zomé," *Anthropologia* 1 (1873):44-58. A discussion of material and nonmaterial aspects of Tupi life.

"The Primordial Inhabitants of Minas Gerais and the Occupations of the Present Inhabitants," *Journal of the Royal Anthropological Institute* 2 (1873):407-423. More evidence of Burton's interest in Brazil.

The Captivity of Hans Stade of Hesse, in A.D. *1547-1555, Among the Wild Tribes of Eastern Brazil. Translated by Albert Tootal, Esq., of Rio de Janeiro, and Annotated by Richard F. Burton.* London: Hakluyt Society, 1874. Cited in Burton's Preface to the poem.

Os Lusíadas (The Lusiads): Englished by Richard Francis Burton. (Edited by His Wife, Isabel Burton). 2 vols. London: Bernard Quaritch, 1880.

Camoens: His Life and His Lusiads. A Commentary by Richard F. Burton (Translator of the Lusiads). 2 vols. London: Bernard Quaritch, 1881.

Iraçema, The Honey-lips. A Legend of Brazil By J. de Alencar. Translated, with the Author's Permission, By Isabel Burton. Manuel de Morais. A Chronicle of the Seventeenth Century By J. M. Pereira da Silva Translated by Richard F. and Isabel Burton. London: Bickers and Son, 1886.

5. Works on Burton and related subjects

(Richards, Alfred Bates, Andrew Wilson [and] St. Clair Baddeley). *A Sketch of the Career of Richard F. Burton. By Alfred Bates Richards, up to 1876, by Andrew Wilson, up to 1879* (and) *by St. Clair Baddeley up to the Present Day.* London: Waterlow and Sons, 1886.

Burton, Isabel. *The Life of Captain Sir Richard F. Burton.* 2 vols. 1893; rpt. Boston: Milford House, 1973. 1:415-454.

Stisted, Georgiana M. *The True Life of Captain Sir Richard F. Burton.* London: H. S. Nichols, 1896, pp. 308-334. This biography by Burton's niece was written in response to Isabel's *Life.* "Miss Stisted . . . says many rather bitter things about Lady Burton that are nevertheless perfectly true" (Penzer, *An Annotated Bibliography,* p. 311).

Wilkins, W. N. *The Romance of Isabel Lady Burton.* 2 vols. London: Hutchinson and Co., 1897. Especially 1:227, 242-243, 264, 340, 345, 348, 352. Wilkins had access to the unpublished manuscript by Lady Burton concerning her journey to Minas Gerais with Sir Richard.

Blunt, Wilfrid Scawen. *My Diaries.* 2 vols. New York: Alfred A. Knopf, 1921. 2:128-131. The author met Lady Burton in Rio and Sir Richard in Buenos Aires.

Penzer, Norman M. *An Annotated Bibliography of Sir Richard Francis Burton.* London: A. M. Philpot, Ltd., 1923. An invaluable work, containing entries for all the editions of Burton's books to 1923 as well as his articles, book reviews, and letters to the press. The manuscript of *The Uruguay* is described on pp. 184-185.

Melo-Leitão, Cândido de. *O Brasil Visto pelos Ingleses.* São Paulo: Companhia Editora Nacional, 1937.

Woodruff, Douglas. *The Tichborne Claimant, a Victorian Mystery.* London: Hollis and Carter, 1957. Burton met the claimant in Buenos Aires and testified at the trial of Tichborne V. Lushington.

Swinburne, Algernon Charles. *The Swinburne Letters,* ed. Cecil Y. Lang. 6 vols. New Haven: Yale University Press, 1959. 1:124, 223, 224. The poet was a close friend of Burton's.

Farwell, Byron. *Burton.* London: Longmans, Ltd., 1963. Especially pp. 293-294; the author obtained a copy of Burton's testimony in the trial of the Tichborne claimant.

Brodie, Fawn M. *The Devil Drives: A Life of Sir Richard Burton.* New York: W. W. Norton and Co., 1967. Pp. 234-246. An unsurpassed biography of Burton.

Garcia, Frederick C. H. "Richard Francis Burton e Luís de Camões: O Tradutor e o Poeta." *Ocidente* (Lisbon), special issue, Nov. 1972, pp. 61-82.

A Catalogue of the Library of Sir Richard Burton, K.C.M.G., held by the Royal Anthropological Institute, ed. by B. J. Kirkpatrick. London: Royal Anthropological Institute, 1979.

6. Other sources

Relação Abreviada da República que os Religiosos Jesuítas das Províncias de Portugal e Espanha Estabeleceram nos Domínios Ultramarinos das Duas Monarquias, e da Guerra que Nele Têm Movido e Sustentado contra os Exércitos Espanhóis e Portugueses: Formada pelos Registos das Secretarias dos Dous Respectivos Principais Comissários e Plenipotenciários; e por Outros Documentos Autênticos. Lisbon, 1757. Also printed in Latin, French, Italian, and German.

Dedução Cronológica e Analítica... Dada à Luz pelo Dr. José Seabra da Silva. 3 vols. Lisbon, 1767. Accusations against the Jesuits, by order of Pombal; it is generally accepted that he wrote part of the book.

Southey, Robert. *History of Brazil.* 3 vols. 1810, 1817, 1819; rpt. New York: Greenwood Press, 1969. 3:465, 471, 478. Known to Burton.

(Cunha, Captain Jacinto Rodrigues da). "Diário da Expedição Gomes Freire de Andrade às Missões do Uruguai, pelo Capitão Jacinto Rodrigues de Andrade, Testemunha Presencial." *Revista do Instituto Histórico e Geográfico Brasileiro* 16 (1853):139-328.

Faria, Jorge de. "Um Século de Teatro Francês em Portugal." *Bulletin d'histoire du théâtre Portugais* 1 (1950):62-92, esp. 77-78. Discusses part of Lisbon's intellectual life in the days of Basílio da Gama.

INDEX